C000181503

Farewell to London's Trolleybuses

Farewell to London's Trolleybuses

MICHAEL H. C. BAKER

IAN ALLAN Publishing

First published 1994

ISBN 0 7110 2281 X

All rights reserved. No part of this book may be
reproduced or transmitted in any form or by any
means, electronic or mechanical, including
photocopying, recording or by any information storage
and retrieval system, without permission from the
Publisher in writing.

© Michael H. C. Baker 1994

Published by Ian Allan Publishing

an imprint of Ian Allan Ltd, Terminal House, Station
Approach, Shepperton, Surrey TW17 8AS.
Printed by Ian Allan Printing Ltd, Coombelands House,
Coombelands Lane, Addlestone, Weybridge, Surrey
KT15 1HY.

Front cover top:
*Stonebridge depot - allocated 'C3' No 289 is caught on
route 662 to Paddington.*

Front cover bottom:
*An impressive line-up in east London sees 'L3' Nó 1391 on
the East Ham circular route 690 and 'N1' No 1592 en route
to Bow Church on the 661.*

Back cover top:
*'Q1' No 1789 heads out of London on the long route 607 to
Uxbridge. This route was converted to bus operation in
November 1960.*

Back cover bottom:
*In pristine condition, 'Q1' No 1830 loads with passengers
prior to departure with a 604 for Kingston.*
All photographs by Julian Thompson.

The lines of John Betjeman's poem *Harrow on the Hill* are
reproduced from his *Collected Poems* by permission of John
Murray (Publishers) Ltd.

Contents

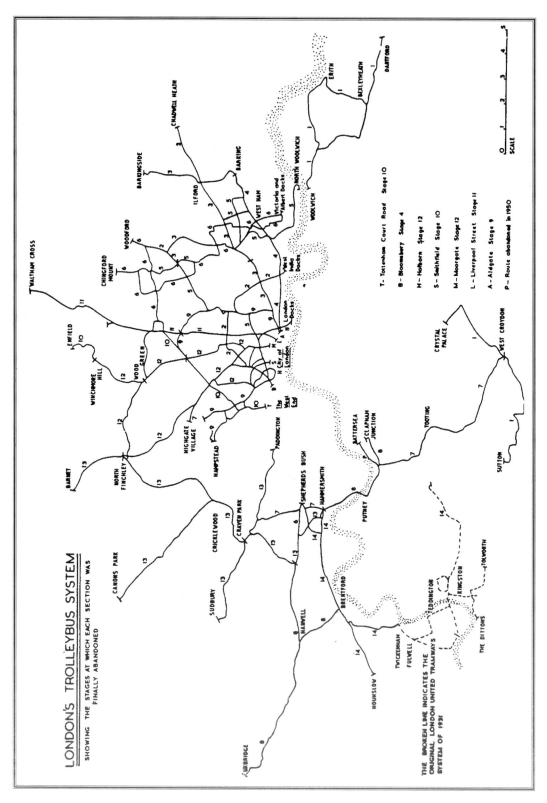

LONDON'S TROLLEYBUS SYSTEM

SHOWING THE STAGES AT WHICH EACH SECTION WAS
FINALLY ABANDONED

T - Tottenham Court Road   Stage 10
B - Bloomsbury   Stage 4
H - Holborn   Stage 12
S - Smithfield   Stage 10
M - Moorgate   Stage 12
L - Liverpool Street   Stage 11
A - Aldgate   Stage 9
P - Route abandoned in 1950

THE BROKEN LINE INDICATES THE
ORIGINAL LONDON UNITED TRAMWAYS
SYSTEM OF 1931

SCALE
0 1 2 3 4 5

Iow was it that the trolleybus, which once
had so bright a future, has quite vanished
from our streets? It might seem to a
generation brought up to regard the environment
as something precious and fragile that an
electrically-powered vehicle capable of carrying
upwards of 70 passengers almost silently would
be the answer to our prayers. The tram, which it
superseded and over which it seemed to have
considerable advantages, is making a vigorous
comeback, and many trolleybus systems are
flourishing overseas. Indeed I made a point of
travelling in an elderly trolleybus in Piraeus and
a new Mercedes articulated example in Zurich
whilst I was gathering material for this book (not
that this was the sole reason for visiting these
cities — I'm not that dedicated!). The Greek
vehicle rattled unmercifully, but then so would a
shipping magnate's Cadillac on the local road
surfaces, whilst the Zurich one hummed
vigorously, especially when accelerating, and
didn't ride as smoothly as the city's modern
trams. Nevertheless the trolleybus clearly has a
future overseas, but there seems little real
possibility of it returning to the streets of any
British city.

The trolleybus network which served London
was the largest in the world. I had watched the
trams disappear between 1950 and 1952 and the
following year borrowed my father's folding
Kodak Brownie for the first time. Once I'd
discovered that, providing there was enough
light, an earthquake wasn't occurring, my finger
wasn't over the lens, and that I had wound the
film on, quite a reasonable picture could result, I
enthusiastically snapped away at anything which
moved, when the pocket money permitted that
was. In 1954 London announced that it would
start to dismantle its trolleybus system in five
years' time. I had missed the trams, but I
determined that I was not going to miss the
trolleys and that I would try to portray a
representative selection of the 1,700-odd vehicles
then in service.

I was still a student when the end came in May
1962. Funds had thus always been limited and I
had been occupied keeping the enemy from our
shores throughout 1956 and 1957 by bashing
away at my World War 2 Imperial typewriter on
behalf of RAF Transport and Fighter Commands.
There were also other distractions, but
nevertheless I had got around the system and I
had accomplished what I had set out to do.

Introduction

That collection forms the basis of this book.
To it I have been able to add pictures from a
number of other sources and, thus, within these
pages we are able to tell in some detail the story
— with a glance back to its beginnings in the
1930s — of the last 10 years of the London
trolleybus from its heyday in the early 1950s,
when the last new vehicles were entering service,
to the final withdrawal in the early hours of
9 May 1962.

When I was growing up in south London in the
1940s the silent streamlined trolleybuses were
not, unlike trams and motorbuses, everyday
transport. I associated them with exotic sounding
places far away to the west and north —
Tolworth, Hounslow and Finchley, for example.
To those not brought up in the London suburbs,
it is almost impossible to convey the sense of
other worldlines of those parts distant from one's
own stamping ground, particularly back in the
days when private motoring was the preserve of
the few. To live north of the Thames seemed to
us south Londoners as alien as inhabiting the far
side of the moon. I had a great aunt who lived in
Pinner. Her rare visits to us involved a journey of
two motor and two trolleybus routes; I thought
this was a tremendous expedition for an elderly
lady to undertake.

When, many years later, I came across John
Betjeman's poem Harrow-on-the-Hill, which is
set within sight of where Aunt May lived and
compares the view at dusk in autumn to that of

the north Cornish coast, I understood just why I found trolleybuses and the places they served so different:

'Then Harrow-on-the-Hill's a rocky island,
And Harrow churchyard full of sailors' graves
And the constant click and kissing of the trolleybuses hissing
Is the level to the Wealdstone turned to waves
And the rumble of the railway
Is the thunder of the rollers
As they gather up for plunging
Into caves.'

Who but Betjeman could have written a poem about London trolleybuses? Mind you, Michael Bentine used to do a very funny act with a sink plunger which concluded with a highly individual impersonation of a trolleybus. Definitely a form of poetry.

It was not that trolleybuses were totally unfamiliar to me. We had two routes in Croydon: the 630 and the 654. I seldom travelled on the latter which ran from Crystal Palace to Sutton, but I did use the 630 from time to time. However, I first got to know trolleybuses really

Above:
One of the pioneer LUT trolleybuses heads down Teddington Road for Kingston through sylvan riverside suburbia in the long-ago days of the 1930s when Al Bowlly caused flappers hearts to flutter and Adolf Hitler could still be dismissed as a figure of fun. I've mentioned earlier that one of our two local routes was the 630. An occasional day out was to Hampton Court. We would travel on the 630 to Hammersmith Broadway and there change on to a 667. I must have first done this at some point during the war. The vehicles which worked the 667 looked identical to those on the 630 but, as we passed through Twickenham, I caught sight of something very different — one of the original Diddlers.

well when we evacuated ourselves to Bournemouth in the last year of the war after a flying bomb had blown away the roof and all the windows of our house. There I travelled every day to school on the 25 which was operated by bright yellow Sunbeam six-wheelers. When, in 1949, I bought my Ian Allan 'abc' of London's trams and trolleybuses I found the very last picture was of just such a trolleybus at work in Barking in 1941. Barking was very exotic and I'd certainly never visited it, but it was interesting to find that Bournemouth trolleys had worked in London.

The Sunbeam company, unlike other trolleybus manufacturers, did not produce motorbuses. This made it distinctive and, therefore, interesting. True, it had become part of the Guy group in 1948, but Sunbeam trolleybuses were amongst the most popular in the country and went on being produced into the 1960s. Yet London never owned any. In the beginning, not surprisingly, AECs were favoured and, when the great tram replacement programme got properly under way in 1935, orders were split between AEC and Leyland. The postwar batches were BUTs, which represented a selling organisation jointly set up by AEC and Leyland. Yet, despite London's trolleybuses being produced by the giants of the diesel and petrol commercial motor business, they were remarkably different from their motorbus compatriots; we shall examine this phenomenon later.

although in neither capital city. In Britain the Railless Electric Traction Co Ltd was set up in 1908 and trials were held in various parts of London before World War 1. For a while nothing came of this in the capital itself but, in the provinces, the trolleybus gradually established itself, at first as an alternative to the tram, which it often resembled, and then, as it developed, as a replacement.

Numerous trolleybus systems were set up during the second and third decades of the 20th century. In the capital the London County Council was the largest operator of trams, and throughout this period it ensured its fleet — the biggest in the country — of some 1,600-odd cars was well-maintained, comfortable and relatively modern. However, other operators serving the capital, or rather its suburbs, either had not the resources of the LCC or the commitment to the tram and by the formation of the London Passenger Transport

Above:
The original LUT trolleybuses were to be withdrawn during the late 1940s. Unlike later trolleybus withdrawals, however, the Diddlers were destined to be replaced by newer trolleybuses. Here a line of withdrawn Diddlers await their fate. V. C. Jones/IAL

The world's first trolleybus, the invention of Dr Ernst Werner von Siemens — still a famous name in electric traction (well the Siemens bit anyway) — ran in Berlin in the spring of 1882. It was 18 years before the experiment was continued, this time in Paris. Trolleybuses still operate in a number of towns and cities in France and Germany,

Board in July 1933 many of their tramcars, and quite often the track they ran on, were worn out. London United Tramways, one of these largely suburban operators, was to be the catalyst for the introduction of trolleybuses to London. It first experimented with them in 1922 and, by the end of the decade when the trolleybus (like the contemporary AEC Regent and Leyland Titan motorbuses) had developed into a comfortable, pneumatic-tyred, covered-top double-decker, had decided to convert its Kingston area services from tram to trolleybus operation. Trolleybus services were inaugurated on 16 May 1931.

Above:
The upper deck of one Diddler found itself serving, after withdrawal, as the 'Locke cafe'. No 1 was preserved and made an appearance on the very last day that trolleybuses operated in London, working out of Fulwell, where it had spent its entire career. Corgi make a rather nice model of it. V. C. Jones/IAL

The 60 trolleybuses, nicknamed, for some long-forgotten reason Diddlers, which the LUT put into service in the Kingston area in 1931 had AEC chassis and were fitted with bodies supplied by the Union Construction & Finance Co Ltd. This company was an offshoot of the Underground group to which the LUT also belonged. Twickenham was the terminus of the 601, one of the routes that the Diddlers traversed, and it was at this location, on a wartime visit to Hampton Court, that the author first saw one of these distinctive vehicles. To one used to the sleek vehicles employed on the 630 and 654 — as well as those employed by Bournemouth Corporation — the lines of the Diddlers looked positively archaic. You can still see for yourself why, as No 1 is now preserved as part of the London Transport Museum Collection.

Superficially the Diddlers looked very like an LT AEC Renown petrol-engined bus; indeed, their chassis had much in common with the Renown, but they lacked the LT-type's well thought out bodywork proportions. The Diddlers also had body design features in common with the 'Feltham' trams, which were built by the same manufacturers and with which they were contemporary. I considered the 'Felthams' the finest tramcars ever, at least until I visited Grenoble in the late 1980s, but their elegant curves were missing from the trolleybuses. The latter somehow contrived to appear both spindly and podgy, particularly around the front end, but in this they were no worse, and in many instances rather better, than contemporary provincial trolleybuses, which in the 1930s were a pretty ill-disposed looking lot.

The Diddlers were classified 'A1' and 'A2' by London Transport. The difference was that the former, Nos 1-35, had English Electric 80hp motors, whilst the latter, Nos 36-60, were fitted with British Thompson-Houston 82hp motors. I've a vague recollection of once travelling on a Diddler, perhaps in the Hampton Court area, as they made the occasional appearance on the 667. All 60 of the type were withdrawn from passenger duties by January 1951.

Three prototypes followed the Diddlers. One of these was ordered by the LUT and the other two by the LPTB. No 61 was delivered in March 1933, some three months before the LPTB came into existence. Classified 'X1', No 61 was an AEC 663T fitted with BTH electrical equipment. It was rebuilt for pay-as-you-enter operation in

The Vehicles

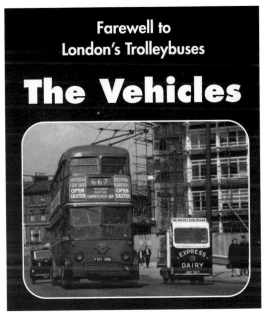

1945. No 61 was very different in appearance to the 'A1s' and 'A2s' and concealed within its elegant body some equally revolutionary features. Its length was increased to 30ft, thus allowing 74 seats — the LCC's standard tram, the 'E/1', seated 71 — and instead of the motor being placed at the front with a bonnet (just like a petrol-engined bus), it was placed under the floor. The body was built by the London General Omnibus Co at its Chiswick Works and was smooth and ultra-modern. Given its parentage No 61 should have resembled an STL, but it is difficult to detect much in common with London's standard double-deck motorbus of the 1930s. It actually looked far more like the prototype double-deck Q1-type motorbus (not the postwar trolleybus design).

No 61 was followed exactly a year later by No 62. This was the true prototype of the London fleet and closely resembled the standard London trolleybus throughout its production run until 1952. It was a superb looking vehicle, one of the truly classic PSV designs. Its clean and elegant lines never dated, so that not only London but other operators were ordering only slightly modified versions after World War 2 and, even at the very end in May 1962, I never heard it suggested that London trolleybuses looked old-fashioned.

No 62, registered AXU188, had 73 seats originally, although this number was later reduced to 70, in an all-metal body built by

Metro-Cammell Weymann. The chassis was an AEC 663T-type, similar to that supplied to No 61. The success of the three-axle vehicle owed much to the chassis design of the earlier LT-type AEC Renown and these elements were perpetuated by later AEC and Leyland deliveries. The all-metal body meant that the lighting had to be of a low voltage and a series of batteries were installed. However, there was also an advantage here, for these batteries could also drive the vehicle for a limited time, around the depot or past an obstruction, at a speed of 4mph.

No 62, like all its successors, was painted by London Transport in its standard red livery, but here the resemblance between the trolleybus and motorbus fleets ended. It has always puzzled me that an organisation which, right from the outset, justly prided itself on standardisation and a corporate image, should have allowed the architecture of its huge fleets of double-deck vehicles to vary so considerably through the 1930s and beyond. No doubt this was because the management of London's trams, and thus the trolleybuses which steadily replaced them during

Above:
No 61, with a Diddler and an East Surrey ST in hot pursuit, is pictured in Kingston prior to the LPTB takeover in July 1933. Ian Allan Library

the 1930s, was by men who had come from a very different tradition from the London General bus world. In The Wheels Used to Talk to Us, the story of Stanley Collins (a London tram driver), the editor (Terence Cooper) writes 'In some curious way the tram and the LCC ethic ... continued within London's tramways and endured almost to the end of trolleybuses in 1962'.

Whereas motorbuses had white-painted window frames on upper and lower-decks, those on trolleybuses were red with pale yellow bands below and above the lower-deck windows. All trolleybuses had rain shields over the windows, no motorbuses did. Yet another difference was that trolleybus fleet numbers corresponded with their registration numbers; motorbuses rarely did. No three-axle double-deck motorbuses were bought by London Transport after the last of the

Above:
The classic lines of the traditional London trolleybus first appeared in early 1934 with the introduction of 'X2' class No 62.

Right:
Put a roofbox STL-type of the late 1930s in its original livery alongside a contemporary trolleybus and, although both were handsome vehicles, you had not got a great deal in common, whether inside or out. No doubt this was another reason why I regarded trolleybuses as exotic, unfamiliar creatures. When the first postwar RTs appeared, I can recall my friend Gillham of class 5 Winterbourne Primary School, SW16, trying to identify them for me — this was before either of us had invested in an 'abc'. 'You mean the ones that look like trolleybuses,' I said. And there was a closer resemblance between a trolleybus and an RT, with its smooth curves and red and cream livery, than there was between the RT and any previous London double-deck bus. Could it be that the trolleybus actually influenced the designers of the RT?

Above left:
This picture, taken in the spring of 1938, perfectly demonstrates the vast difference between the standard 'E/1' type tram, dating back originally before World War 1, with its front and rear platforms open to the elements, and the ultra-modern, streamlined trolleybus. The 617 began operating on 6 March 1938, whilst tram route 3 was replaced by trolleybuses on 10 July that year. London Transport

Left:
Crowds boarding a trolleybus in Silvertown Way, Canning Town, in December 1941. London Transport

Above:
'D3' trolleybus No 514 stands at the Battersea terminus of the 612.
V. C. Jones/IAL

Right:
The 612 had been introduced as 'half a service' in September 1937, when trolleybuses had arrived at Wandsworth and Hammersmith depots and tram route 12, which ran from London Bridge to Tooting, was cut back to serve the inner London section from Wandsworth to London Bridge. The 612 covered the outer part from Battersea (Princes Head) to Mitcham Fair Green. From that date until 1950, Wandsworth depot had housed both trams and trolleybuses. From 1 October 1950 the through connection between London Bridge and Tooting, lost in 1937, was restored by bus service 44. This was actually an improvement, at both ends, as the trams had only got as far as Borough, which was not quite London Bridge, whilst the southern terminus of the 44, as of the replaced 612, was Mitcham. An inspector checks all is well at the Wandsworth terminus of tram route 12; in the distance is an 'E/3' tram. The trolleybus overhead can be seen above the tram stop. V. C. Jones/IAL

LT-type in November 1932, although the AEC Renown was available until the war — Leicester Corporation, for example, put some 64-seaters into service in 1939. Completely different destination layouts were chosen, the trolleybuses displaying the route number above a rather large indicator for the 'via' and destination points compared to the three-indicator arrangements of motorbuses. I can think of no other operator which thus distinguished between its trolley and motorbus fleets. Moreover, motorbuses carried the garage code and running number but, until the 1950s, trolleybuses carried only a number.

And another thing; whilst not one of the main body and chassis alterations carried out on the long-based Regent from 1952 until well into the war — and beyond (except for the RTs) — disqualified the vehicle from being designated 'STL', the smallest trolleybus variation — an additional locker, brake modification, the substitution of stilton for cheddar in the driver's sandwiches it almost seemed — warranted a new classification. By the date of the introduction of the 'Q1s' in 1948, London Transport had a grand total of 42 different classes of trolleybus — not bad for a fleet of 1,764.

The third experimental trolleybus was No 63, which entered service in 1934. This was an AEC 661T fitted with English Electric bodywork. Classified 'X3', No 63 was destined to be the only two-axle trolleybus in the London fleet. Both Nos 62 and 63 were acquired at a time when the LPTB was seeking powers to convert routes to trolleybus operation. Acts were obtained in 1934, 1935 and 1936 for the conversion of 200 route miles, whilst a further act of 1937 allowed for the conversion of the remainder of the system. From 1935 onwards, bulk deliveries of trolleybuses were made as the conversion programme took effect. By the early years of the war the London fleet had expanded to a total of more than 1,700 vehicles. The post-1935 deliveries can be summarised as follows, see right:

Type	Fleet Numbers	Chassis	Body	To service
B1	64-93	Leyland	BRCW	1935-6
B2	94-131	Leyland	Brush	1935
C1	132-41	AEC 664T	Weymann	1935
C1	142-83	AEC 664T	MCW	1935
C2	184-283	AEC 664T	MCW	1936
C3	284-383	AEC 664T	BRCW	1936/7
D1	384	Leyland	Leyland	1936
D2	385-483	Leyland	MCW	1936/7
B3	484-88	Leyland	BRCW	1936
B1	489-93	Leyland	BRCW	1936
D3	494-553	Leyland	BRCW	1937
E1	554-603	AEC 664T	Brush	1937
E2	604-28	AEC 664T	Weymann	1937
E3	629-53	AEC 664T	Park Royal	1937
F1	654-753	Leyland	Leyland	1937
X4	754	LPTB/AEC	LPTB	1937
H1	755-904	Leyland	MCW	1938
J1	905-52	AEC 664T	Weymann*	1938
N1	953	AEC/MCW	Weymann	1938
L2	954	MCW/AEC	MCW	1938
J2	955-1029	AEC 664T	BRCW	1938
J3	1030-54	AEC 664T	BRCW	1938
K1	1055-154	Leyland	Leyland	1938/9
K2	1155-254	Leyland	Leyland	1938/9
K1	1255-304	Leyland	Leyland	1938/9
K2	1305-54	Leyland	Leyland	1938/9
L1	1355-69	MCW/AEC	MCW	1939
L2	1370-78	MCW/AEC	MCW	1939
X5	1379	Chassisless	MCW	1939
L3	1380-529	AEC/MCW	MCW	1939/40
M1	1530-54	AEC/MCW	Weymann	1939/40
N1	1555-644	AEC 664T	BRCW	1939/40
N2	1645-69	AEC 664T	Park Royal	1939/40
X6	1670	EE/AEC	EE	1940
X7	1671	Chassisless	Leyland	1939
K3	1672-96	Leyland	Leyland	1940
P1	1697-721	Leyland	MCW	1941

* 952 bodied by MCW

Left:
Over the years the 44 has been cut back at both ends until, by 1994, it was very nearly back to where the 612 used to run. All that was left was the extension from Battersea to Vauxhall, the section thence to London Bridge being covered by the 344. More than four decades after the demise of the trolleybuses, Metrobus M830 sets off from Vauxhall on a mild, February morning in 1994.

Above:
*'C1' class No 147, one of the vehicles displaced by the new
'Q1' class and subsequently withdrawn in March 1955,
stands at the Hounslow terminus of the 657.* V. C. Jones/IAL

Below:
*Withdrawn in March 1955, 'C1' No 169, of Highgate depot,
speeds through King's Cross.* London Transport

If the war had not intervened all of London's trams would have been replaced by trolleybuses, for a bill to this effect was introduced in Parliament in 1937 and was enacted. The outbreak of war did not bring conversions to an immediate halt. Many expected immediate devastation from the air and, when this failed to materialise, things reverted to a degree of normality. This 'Phoney War' lasted until the summer of 1940. The Blitz began in early July and the first damage to be inflicted on London Transport was when the trolleybus wires were brought down in New Malden on 16 August that year, although it was the east London routes, close to the docks, which were to receive the full brunt of the Luftwaffe's attack.

Meanwhile trams had continued to give way to trolleybuses, chiefly in east London. Hackney, Bow, West Ham and Poplar depots were all converted and trams went forever from the heart of the East End and Docklands — although I suppose it might be argued that something like them returned with the opening of the Docklands Light Railway. The vehicles, Leylands and AECs of course, were built to prewar standards, although the last, No 1721, was not delivered

Farewell to London's Trolleybuses
The
Wartime Years

Below:
'B2' type No 126, withdrawn in October 1952, is seen in Camden Town shortly before withdrawal whilst on its way to Hampstead Heath. The trolleybus appears to be in some sort of trouble for, despite its fairly full complement of passengers, it has its poles down. V. C. Jones/IAL

until 1 October 1941, more than two years after the outbreak of war. The last conversions of the immediate programme occurred on 9 June 1940 when three new trolleybus service were inaugurated. These were the 565 (Holborn-East Ham), the 567 (Aldgate-Barking) and the 665 (Bloomsbury-Barking). By this date the trolleybuses operated over some 250 route miles; the trams, in contrast, had contracted to around 100 route miles primarily south of the Thames.

By the end of the war some 17 trolleybuses had been destroyed — 'B2' No 99, 'C3' No 364, 'D2s' Nos 386/87/94/98, 418/28/35/48, 'H1s' Nos 787/91, 812, the unique 'N1' No 953, 'L1' No 1365, 'L3s' Nos 1387/492 — and a further 61 were rebodied. A total of 16 were treated by Weymann (Nos 95, 107, 406, 621, 792/95, 803/61, 1001/123/128/244/247/285/565/587) in 1941/42. These vehicles had their fleet numbers suffixed by 'A' and were also reclassified. A total of 25 passed through East Lancs between 1945 and 1948 — Nos 390-92/95, 405/07/09/12/51/70, 766/84/86/90/94/99, 801/04/08, 993, 1001A/007/385/543/545. The fleet numbers on these 25 were suffixed 'B' and were likewise reclassified. Finally, 20 were treated by Northern Counties in 1946 and were renumbered and reclassified with the suffix 'C'. These were Nos 97/98, 385/89/96/97, 402/15/19/30, 575, 78, 602/23/26/29/33/35/41/43.

A total of a further 43 new vehicles had also been delivered during the war years. These comprised three batches of vehicles diverted from orders placed by Durban (SA1 and SA2) and Johannesburg (SA3) in South Africa:

Type	Fleet Numbers	Chassis	Body	To service
SA1	1722-33	Leyland	MCW	1941/2
SA2	1734-46	Leyland	MCW	1942
SA3	1747-64	AEC 664T	MCW	1942/3

Below:
No 1671 was another unique experimental vehicle. Built by Leyland initially as a demonstrator, it passed to the LPTB in 1939. It was unusual in having two front axles and only one at the rear. The theory behind this was that such an arrangement would reduce wear and tear on the tyres caused by tight corners. It was to remain in service until May 1955. It is seen on the forecourt of Fulwell depot. V. C. Jones/IAL

Above:
Prototype Routemaster RM1 made its public début in September 1954. Many modifications later it is pictured working 'under the wires' at Golders Green on 7 February 1956. London Transport

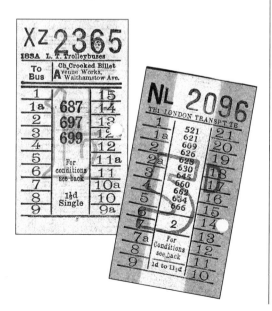

On the last day of 1946 the total of trolleybuses in service with London Transport had reached 1,747, making it the largest single fleet in the world. The first of the postwar generation of trolleybuses was ordered in 1946 (although the first deliveries were not received until 1948), but those who fondly imagined that these would herald the renewal of the tramway replacement programme were sadly disappointed for, on 15 November that year, London Transport announced that diesel buses, being 'eminently suitable and much cheaper', would take the place of the remaining 800-odd trams. So trolleybuses would never pose, as generations of trams and motorbuses have done, on Westminster Bridge beneath Big Ben, nor monopolise the Embankment, reach the West End at Victoria nor come within sight of St Paul's on the northern approaches to Southwark Bridge. Despite the construction of a test vehicle, trolleybuses were destined never to operate in service through the Kingsway subway; the type would always be a suburbanite.

London and its suburbs are vast. To an outsider the suburbs may well seem an almost limitless, unplanned sprawl, with little of architectural merit or fame, except perhaps, here and there, the name of a familiar football league club, peopled by a mass of humanity, living, working, buying, selling, worshipping and entertaining itself, with which he has no connection. But it is not really like this. The truth is that each part is different and subtly distinctive, a complex structure of communities, changing but often with deep routes, linked on many levels and in many ways which the stranger may sometimes stumble upon and perhaps become part of.

The transport network forms part of this and, to the outsider, there may appear to be little rhyme or reason why a particular route starts where it does, twists and turns, and eventually terminates nowhere in particular. The classic example of this was the 630 destination 'Near Willesden Junction'. When the time came to abolish the trolleys many routes did change. Many were extended, particularly into the West End proper, and were amalgamated with existing motorbus routes. This was because the needs and locations of populations had changed; indeed, these inevitable shifts were one of the principal downfalls of the inflexible trolleybus network. Yet some traffic flows have remained constant over decades and the motorbuses which operate them follow many of the same roads and streets

Above left:
Bexleyheath operated a particularly interesting group of vehicles, less standardised than at any other London depot. There were two reasons for this. Originally short-wheelbased 60-seaters had been used; typical of these is 'B2' No 105 seen amongst the trilby hats and cloth caps at the Woolwich terminus when new in October 1935. However, traffic grew rapidly and longer 70-seaters were drafted in. Secondly, in 1941 and again in 1944, air raids wiped out or badly damaged most of the depot's allocation. This meant a hasty rounding-up of surplus vehicles from elsewhere. These were later joined by some of the survivors of the Blitz and Doodlebugs. These survivors had either been heavily rebuilt or had been completely rebodied.

Left:
The Woolwich area was the last in London where trams and trolleybuses could be seen operating together. The 40 was one of London's very last tram routes, being converted to bus operation in July 1952 during the final stage of 'Operation Tramaway'. 'E/1' No 1833 changes from overhead to conduit in Woolwich beside the Free Ferry Bakery, whilst a trolleybus draws up behind the ancient Morris Minor van and a brand-new RT on route 75 gets ready to head back to West Croydon. V. C. Jones/IAL

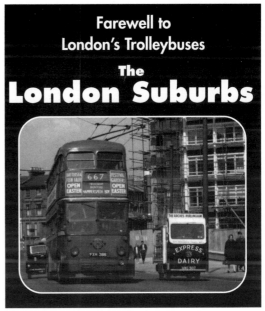

Farewell to London's Trolleybuses

The London Suburbs

as did their electrically-powered predecessors, both trolleybuses and trams. This is one reason why, today, the tram is flourishing all over Europe and making a comeback in Britain.

I have said that I first associated trolleybuses with west and north London. It was somewhat later that I made the acquaintance of those in the east. London east of the cities of Westminster and London was and is very different to the suburbs in the west. When we think of the East End I guess we think of Cockneys born within the sound of Bow Bells — which carry rather further than the ringing of the tram, trolleybus and motorbus bells of the generations of vehicles which have lived in Bow depot and garage — and the Docks. I first got to know the East End from the river when each year we would take a trip aboard an Eagle paddle steamer from Tower Pier, past Wapping, Shadwell, Limehouse, Greenwich, Blackwall and Woolwich — then the world's busiest docks — beyond the P&O liners at Tilbury to the world's longest pier. Much later I worked there, at an FE college between the Commercial and Whitechapel roads.

West London is more modern, art deco factories built between the wars, Wembley stadium and semi-detached houses with rising sun motifs on their garage gates; the East End was older, Dickensian, a mix of many nationalities and all dominated by vast warehouses, cranes and ships' masts. Tall, rattling trams, jostling on the cobbled streets with horse-drawn drays, costers and charabancs bound for Southend and Clacton, seemed somehow more appropriate than the almost silent, sleek trolleybuses.

East and west have changed in the 30 or so years since the trolleybus disappeared. One-way traffic schemes and pedestrianised or bus-only town centres have flourished. No one needs to be reminded of the dramatic decline and death of London Docks, replaced by Docklands, that visually spectacular, socially divisive monument to the 1980s, the Thatcher-inspired decade of individual and corporate greed. Here and there, odd fragments of the old world — one in which there was certainly room for improvement — survive: a few cranes; the industries along Silvertown Road along which the 699 route ran; a towering, reinforced-concrete Co-op warehouse; the empty docks themselves. Ethnically, the area is as mixed as ever. So now, in places, is west London, although in other respects the changes there are less dramatic. More and larger jet airliners than the 707s and Viscounts of the 1960s fly over it, trolley and motorbuses are no longer built at Southall, Park Royal or Chiswick, but there are less of the disastrous high-rise developments which afflicted the East End and many of the suburban avenues seem little changed.

Below:
Two 'D2s' are pictured outside Dartford town hall.
Dartford Public Libraries

WOOLWICH
PLUMSTEAD
WICKHAM LANE
WELLING CORNER

696

BEXLEYHEATH
CRAYFORD
WEST HILL
DARTFORD

PLUMSTEAD
ABBEY WOOD
ERITH
BARNEHURST

698

Although the LPTB confirmed that it intended to convert its remaining tram routes to motorbus operation shortly after the end of the war, it was not until 1950 that the conversion programme, codenamed 'Operation Tramaway', was put into effect. Stage One of the programme took place on 1 October 1950. The relevance of this to the story of the final decade of London's trolleybuses is that, apart from the abandonment of six tram routes (including one all-night service) in the Battersea and Wandsworth area, a single trolleybus route — the 612 — was also converted to bus operation. The 14 'D3' trolleybuses, which had lived at Wandsworth since new, all survived their replacement by diesel buses and were transferred away to Walthamstow. Wandsworth thus became the second depot in London to lose its allocation of trolleybuses, following from Acton which had ceased to house trolleybuses before the outbreak of World War 2.

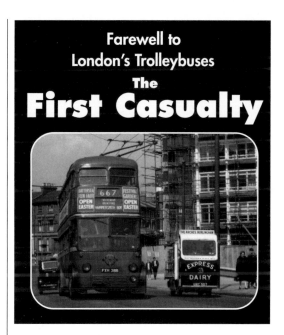

Farewell to
London's Trolleybuses

The

First Casualty

Left:
Two routes were operated by Bexleyheath depot: the 696 and the 698 (as shown on this blind). The former was replaced, neatly, by the 96 bus route, but there was no direct replacement for the 698. Ian Allan Library

Below:
As with all conversion schemes a number of existing motorbus routes were affected at the same time. These could be strengthened, diverted, lengthened or, occasionally, curtailed. The 229 was extended from Bexleyheath to Woolwich to cover the abandoned 698. A scene in Abbey Wood garage some years later sees RT1586 on route 229, alongside RM604 on the 21 and RM8 on the 228. The last of the trio, although the first production RM, had only just entered service after spending no less than 15 years as Chiswick's experimental vehicle.

Above:
Unlike the victims of all subsequent replacement stages, those vehicles withdrawn after the conversion of the 696 and 698 were taken to the Penhall Road, Charlton, yard where a decade earlier the last trams had met their end. A group of withdrawn trolleybuses, seen in varying degrees of dereliction, await their fate on 20 April 1959. The four nearest the camera are: 'C2' No 187, 'J2' No 97c, 'K3' No 1690 and 'F1' No 711. No 97c had been rebodied by Northern Counties in 1946, whilst No 1690 should not really have been there at all. This was one of the last prewar designed vehicles to be delivered and was an all-Leyland that entered service in November 1940. It had been allocated to, and remained at, Edmonton until withdrawal in September 1958; presumably it had developed a fault considered too costly to rectify at so late a stage in its career and had therefore been withdrawn. It was the first of its class to be taken out of service.

Left:
A group of us art students visited Penhall Road several times to sketch the trolleybuses and — I fear — assist in their demolition. Harry Isles — now a doting grandfather — takes a swing at 'D2'

On the vehicle front, delivery of the first batch of 'Q1s' had been completed in March 1949. A second batch commenced delivery in the spring of 1952 and at Christmas that year London's very last trolleybus, No 1891 (LYH891), arrived. The fleet total now stood at its highest ever total — 1,811. Trolleybuses operated over one fifth of the service mileage of the Central Road Services — a department within which they had been absorbed in 1950. Yet the decline had already set in.

Thirty standard prewar trolleybuses were taken out of service in 1952/53. Amongst these was the entire short-wheelbase 'B2' class, apart from No 99 (which had been destroyed in the bombing of Bexleyheath depot in June 1944) and the four rebodied vehicles (Nos 95A, 97C, 98C and 107A). This quartet soldiered on until the late 1950s; one was withdrawn in 1958, the remaining three in 1959. The remainder of the withdrawals in 1952 were 13 'D3s'.

Only one trolleybus, 'C3' No 378 was withdrawn in 1954, but 1955 was a watershed for public transport. A number of factors contributed to this. Britain was well into the postwar boom; Harold MacMillan, the Prime Minister who was to tell us we'd never had it so good, would come to power after the Suez Crisis of 1956; and between 1950 and 1955 private car ownership had risen by 67%. Congestion, as a glance at any postcard of London Bridge, Mansion House or Ludgate Circus in pre-motorcar days will confirm, had existed from mid-Victorian times in some parts of the capital. But, by the mid-1950s, it was growing and spreading. Unemployment was virtually non-existent in London and the southeast. The once highly esteemed status of the bus driver was declining, with the result that London Transport was starting to have trouble in recruiting staff and seemed unable, or unwilling, to maintain competitive wage levels. Fares were increased twice in 1955; the population in central London and the inner suburbs was in decline.

Public transport in London had been expanding for over 100 years but now the trend was downwards. Successive service cuts in February, March, May and June 1955 meant that by the end of the year 5% of London's motor and trolleybuses were permanently out of work. A total of 135 trolleybuses were withdrawn during the year: 17 in February, 58 in March, 36 in May and 24 in June. Amongst the casualties was the five strong 'B3' class (Nos 484-88), although the

Developments during the 1950s

five 'B1s' also built in September 1936 (Nos 489-93), and identical except for having coasting and run-back brakes, soldiered on until the final slaughter in 1959-62. Amongst the rest of the withdrawals were two of the earlier, CGF-registered 'B1s', 35 'C1s', 30 'C2s', 10 'C3s', seven 'E1s', and four of the experimental trolleybuses: Nos 754, 1670 (both chassisless), 1379 (the Kingsway Subway trolleybus) and 1671 (the unique twin-axle steering vehicle).

Although the reduction in passenger journeys on trolleybuses steepened in 1956 to 8%, withdrawals were considerable fewer than in 1955 — a total of 41 in all. These withdrawals comprised examples of the 'C', 'D' and 'E' classes, along with 'N2' class No 1662, which was burned out whilst undergoing overhaul at Charlton works in August.

Nearly all the withdrawn vehicles took a one-way trip to Bird's scrapyard on the northern edge of Stratford-upon-Avon. A few were also broken up by Thompsons of Cardiff, whilst five 'C1s' (Nos 138/42/48/75/83) were to be exported to Georgetown Municipal Transport (Penang, Malaysia). These five were withdrawn in 1959 and scrapped in Malaysia by the far-eastern branch of a firm that was to feature heavily in the disposal of London's remaining trolleybuses — George Cohen.

In 1957 the reduction in trolleybus journeys was less marked — at 3.7% — and London Transport as a whole made a profit for the first time since 1948. It might appear remarkable to younger readers that 824 trolleybuses were scheduled for operation on Christmas Day 1957. A mere 10 trolleybuses were withdrawn during the year: Nos 263/70/74/83, 385C, 490, 572, 795A, 803A, 1244A. The London firm of George Cohen, based at Colindale, featured in the list of dealers now breaking up redundant vehicles, many of them those withdrawn the previous year.

If 1957 had seemed to be resisting the downward trend in public transport patronage, then 1958 left no one in doubt that downward it most definitely was. London Transport as a whole earned nearly £4 million less during the year than in 1957. In the first quarter passenger journeys were down by 7%. In late March a long-running pay dispute came to a head and a few days later notice was given that the Transport & General Workers Union would call a strike in a month's time. The strike duly started on Sunday 4 May. For week after week the streets of London saw no buses (apart from a few emergency services, mostly operated by the maverick People's League for the Defence of Freedom), Green Line coaches or trolleybuses. The strike lasted seven weeks. Coincidentally on 25 June, four days after services were resumed, a revised trolleybus schedule was introduced with a reduction in requirements of 36 vehicles on Mondays to Fridays. Fares went up on all motor and trolleybus services on 10 August in an attempt to recoup some of the losses. This was only a sticking plaster measure for many passengers never returned and massive service reductions, including the withdrawal of complete routes, followed. In all, 20% fewer passengers were carried on London Transport road services in 1958 compared to the previous year.

Ironically the cuts in trolleybus services were not introduced until 7 January 1959 (services abandoned on 6 January included the 664 from Paddington to Edgware but all the sections affected were covered by other services); it had been the intention that the programme to eliminate finally the trolleybuses would begin on 1 January 1959, but production delays meant that there was a reprieve of two months. Nevertheless, 58 trolleybuses were taken out of service at the end of that first week. In a few months' time the loss of a mere 58 vehicles would seem to be almost nothing in comparison with the subsequent wholesale slaughter which would continue until the London trolleybus became history.

Below:
Three days after I photographed the line-up, No 970 met its end. Wreathed in smoke from the flames which will soon consume it, No 97c topples over.

On 3/4 March 1959 the beginning of the end, postponed many times, at last arrived. For several years the continual decline in passengers meant that London Transport had more double-deck buses of the RT family than it needed and in 1955 it had been proposed to use some of these to replace the Bexleyheath and Carshalton trolleybuses. However, at that time, economics decreed that the surplus motorbuses be sold — they were rapidly snapped up and saw many years of further service in places like Dundee, where they ironically helped seal the fate of the city's tramway network — and the trolleybuses were kept running. It was then expected that the purpose-designed trolley replacement diesel bus, the Routemaster, would be well into its production run by the beginning of 1958. It wasn't; nor was it a year later.

By the autumn of 1958 London Transport decided that surplus RTs would, after all, be used to replace the trolleybuses based at Carshalton and Bexleyheath depots. These had been chosen for two main reasons: Carshalton because it was operating the oldest vehicles in the fleet — the 23-year old 'B1s' — and Bexleyheath because it was physically separated from the rest of the system.

A total of 34.45 miles of overhead was abandoned as a result of this first stage. The only section shared with other routes was the 0.8 miles through Croydon from Old Town, where the Archbishops of Canterbury used to maintain their summer residence, to West Croydon station which the trolleybuses on route 654 worked along with those on London's longest route, the 630.

Converted to trolleybus operation on 10 November 1935 the 696 — Dartford-Woolwich Ferry via Welling — and the 698 — Bexleyheath-Woolwich Ferry via Abbey Wood — were largely replacements for tram services inherited from Bexleyheath UDC and Dartford Council (which had merged their operations during World War 1). The original tram services were numbered 96 and 98; the latter originally terminated at Abbey Wood forcing through passengers to change. One of the immediate benefits of the new trolleybus service was that the necessity for this change was removed. Such was the success of the trolleybus services that the original 60-seat vehicles were soon replaced by the 70-seat 'H1s'. In one of the

Farewell to London's Trolleybuses

Stage...

3/4 March 1959

1

most damaging raids on London Transport during World War 2, 27 trolleybuses and eight trams were destroyed by a raid on Bexleyheath depot in November 1940. This depot is of interest in as much as it was the only purpose-built trolleybus depot constructed for the 1930s conversion programme.

The 654, which was converted from Sutton to West Croydon on 8 December 1935 and extended to Crystal Palace on 9 February 1936, replaced part of the tramway network inherited by the LPTB from the South Met, one of the other constituents of the 'UndergrounD' group (which also included the MET and LUT). The route to Crystal Palace was notorious for possessing one of the steepest gradients — 1 in 9 — on a London trolleybus route — Anerley Hill. As a result the trolleybuses for this service were fitted with run-back brakes and one of these, No 65, was used in tests on the hill before services were inaugurated. An additional five 'B1s', Nos 489-93, were acquired in 1936 to supplement those already available. A total of 21 trolleybuses was required to operate the weekday service, with 26 on Saturdays. One of the factors in the decision to convert this route early in the abandonment programme was the age of the vehicles used. The last trolleybus in service on the 654 was 'B1' No 83, which was then almost 25 years old.

Route Nos	Terminals	Replacement route	Type of Vehicle	Remarks
654	Crystal Palace-Sutton	154	RT	
696	Woolwich-Dartford	96	RT	195 introduced
698	Woolwich-Bexleyheath	229	RT	

The following bus routes were amended: 64, 124, 132, 157, 229

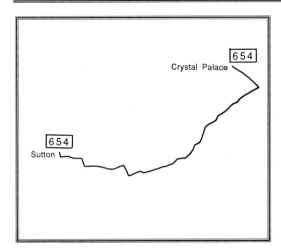

Below:
Isolated though the Bexleyheath routes were from the rest of the trolleybus system, they were separated only by the width of the River Thames from the North Woolwich terminus of the 569 and 669 and vehicles requiring attention at Charlton Works were taken across the river on the Woolwich Free Ferry. A telephoto view from North Woolwich on 22 February 1994 of the ferry shows a Bexleyheath DMS on the 96 and an RT on the 229.

Above right:
Strangely there were reminders of trolleybuses at that time in Woolwich for a number of preserved PSVs, including ex-Huddersfield No 541 (a three-axle Karrier), were stored there. It is seen standing next to an RT in March 1978.

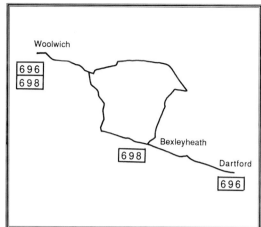

Above:
The 654 had replaced the former South Metropolitan trams which ran between Sutton and West Croydon on 9 December 1935. It was extended to Crystal Palace two months later. A couple of these ancient four-wheelers, with a scarcely more modern vehicle on the 30, are seen in Tamworth Road with the tower of Croydon parish church in the background.
Lens of Sutton

Above left:

The 30 members of the short-wheelbase 'B1' class were always associated with the 654; indeed only two would appear ever to have worked elsewhere and then but briefly. They were fitted with coasting and run-back brakes to prevent any nasty moments on the climb up to Crystal Palace. The second of the class, No 65, a Leyland with BRCW bodywork dating from November 1935, is seen in Tamworth Road, pursued by a 'P1' class on the 630 in August 1954. The view is taken from more or less the same location as the previous illustration, but looking up the hill towards West Croydon. No 65 had been the vehicle used for trial runs on Anerley Hill leading up to Crystal Palace during the winter of 1935/36. When the Crystal Palace itself burned down on the night of 30 November 1936 crowds from all over London came to view the fearsome spectacle. However, the trolleybuses on the 654 were unable to reach their terminus and were forced to turn at the bottom of the hill in Penge. No 65 was chosen for the official last run of the 654 on the night of Tuesday 3 March 1959. It carried various local dignitaries and was conducted by M. L. Lambert, who had begun his career with Croydon Corporation in 1919.

Left:

It is 18 February 1959 and the penultimate member of the 'B1' class, No 92, speeds past the West Croydon terminus of the 75. This was the route which linked the Carshalton and the Bexleyheath trolleybus routes — where RT2924 rests. Unlike most London trolleybuses, No 92 retained its original mesh ventilation grille right to the end.

Above:

West Croydon pictured on the last day of the 654 — a wet 3 March 1959. Latterly the 1938 batch of 'B1s', Nos 489-93, had worked this route. No 491, on its way to Sutton, passes one of the original 1935 batch heading for the Palace. Godstone and Catford RTs, a Morris Minor and an Austin Cambridge complete the cast. The pole on the traffic island in the right foreground is the one around which the trolleybuses on route 630 circumnavigated as they set off for 'Near Willesden Junction'.

Above:
The next day, 4 March 1959, the streets have dried, the 630's loop of wires remains, but the crew of the AEC Mercury tower wagon have already removed those for the 654 as replacement RT3264 eases past. The latter is one of many newly-overhauled roof-box RTs allocated to Carshalton. The 157 was not a new route but was extended from Wallington over the former 654 route to Crystal Palace and was worked both by Merton garage (AL) as before and by Carshalton. There are even more RTs in this picture than the previous one; the inevitable Morris Minor has also managed to sneak its nose in.

Left:
Nominally the oldest of the 23 scheduled RTs allocated to Carshalton was RT181 seen here outside the garage on 12 March 1959. Although it has a roof-box body, it is a slightly later one than its original, 1947-built, Park Royal example. The 154 was a straight replacement of the 654, extended beyond its Sutton terminus to Morden.

We now move across the river to east London and Stage Two which saw the end of trolleybuses from Clapton and Lea Bridge depots. The RMs were still not ready, but none of the three routes involved — the 555, the 581 and the 677 — were in a healthy financial position and London Transport wanted to substitute diesel buses as soon as possible. 14 April 1959 was the last day of operation for these services.

Two of the three routes had their origins in joint tram services operated between Leyton Corporation and the LCC. The 555, which linked Bloomsbury with Leyton, and the 581, from Bloomsbury to Woodford, were both converted to trolleybus operation on 11 June 1939. Electric trams in Leyton first operated in December 1906, but it was not until 1910 that services were extended beyond the borough boundary over LCC metals to Bloomsbury. Under the 1913 allocation of route numbers the Bloomsbury-Leyton service became route 55, whilst the alternative Bloomsbury-Leyton service introduced in 1915 became service 81. As a result of problems, the LCC took over the management and operation of Leyton's tramway network in 1921 on a 10-year arrangement and in early March 1931 tram route No 81 was

Farewell to London's Trolleybuses

Stage... 2
14/15 April 1959

Right:
'K1' No 1290 of Lea Bridge depot is caught at the Bloomsbury terminus of route 555 on the last day of May 1957. This terminus was, arguably, the nearest the trolleybuses reached to the West End. I know I was not a little surprised on the warm early summer morning of this picture on taking a slight diversion from Oxford Street where it crosses Kingsway — I was probably on my way to pressing my nose against Bassett Lowke's window in High Holborn — to come across a trolleybus so far away from the suburbs which were its natural habitat. No 1290 belonged to the largest group of London trolleybuses, the 'K1' and 'K2' classes. There were 300 of these all-Leyland vehicles built between October 1938 and June 1939. Half of them, of which No 1290 was an example, were fitted with Metrovick controllers and classified K1; the 'K2s' were identical except for their English Electric controllers.

As a result of their relative modernity, few 'K1s' and 'K2s' were scrapped in the initial stages of the trolleybus replacement programme. Instead, they moved around the ever-shrinking network, rather like mourners at a series of wakes, their numbers steadily decreasing. Some survived until the very end, working from Isleworth depot. No 1290 was one of these, working the 657 until the last day of London trolleybuses on 8 May 1962, after which it was towed to Colindale for breaking up. The Stage Two abandonment and the dispersal of the 'K1s' and 'K2s' meant the end of the 'D2' and 'D3' classes.

extended to Woodford. The conversion of these two routes represented one of the final stages in the conversion of the east London tramway network to trolleybus operation.

The final route converted at this stage was the 677 which linked Smithfield with the West India Docks. It had been converted to trolleybus operation on 10 September 1939 from tram route No 77, with the inner terminus being transferred from Aldersgate to Smithfield. The 77 was one of the last LCC tram routes to be introduced, dating originally to 1913 when a shuttle between Dalston Lane and Hackney station was introduced. Extensions later saw the service operate from West India Docks to Aldersgate from December 1921.

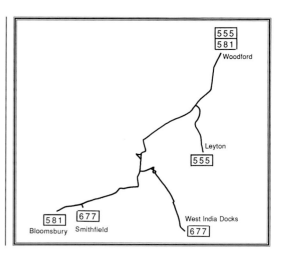

Route Nos	Terminals	Replacement route	Type of Vehicle	Remarks
555	Bloomsbury-Leyton	170	RTL	
581	Bloomsbury-Woodford	38a	RTL	
677	Smithfield-West India Docks	277	RTL	

The following bus route were amended: 56

Below left:

Although the present day terminus of the 277 is not far from what was the West India Docks, all is utterly changed. A Titan of the East London division of London Buses is seen there at dusk on 29 December 1993. The bus looks toylike, dwarfed by the Cabot Tower at Canary Wharf — the tallest building in the United Kingdom.

Right:

The 38a has long disappeared, but the 38 is still crew-operated with Routemasters. The lowest-numbered production RM and the oldest still in service, RM5, which was under construction at the time of the 555/581/677 conversion, is seen taking a day off from its Clapton home on a trip to the seaside for the 1993 Historic Commercial Club Vehicle run to Brighton.

Below:

Only one new route, the 277, was needed for the Clapton and Lea Bridge replacement programmes, the rest being provided by an extension of the tram replacement service 170 and, particularly, by greatly strengthening the 38 and 38s routes. Former Country Area RT974, transferred to Leyton garage, stands at the Victoria terminus of the 38 in 1970. A total of 99 buses (67 RTLs and 32 RTs) replaced 84 trolleybuses.

Above:
Conversation piece in front of the trolleybuses and the RTLs which were about to replace them. Fox Photos

Below:
Two 'SA3s', with No 1758 leading, stand in sunny Barking one afternoon in 1954. The 'SAs' were restricted to the local routes operated by Ilford depot and, therefore, never in normal circumstances penetrated or closely approached the City of London. V. C. Jones/IAL

Stage three saw diesel buses, but still not Routemasters, replacing trolleybuses at Bow and Ilford depots on 18 August 1959. A total of four routes — Nos 661, 663, 691 and 693 — were converted at this time. Amongst the casualties at this stage were the remaining vehicles of those diverted from orders originally placed by Durban and Johannesburg in South Africa which had been delivered between 1941 and 1943. London was one of a number of places to benefit from vehicles of this nature, which were desperately needed to make up for wartime losses in the capital.

A total of 43 vehicles originally formed the three classes of the 'SA' type. Ten had been withdrawn before the conversion of these routes. The three batches utilised Leyland and AEC chassis and were all fitted with MCW bodywork. So far they sound pretty standard, but they were also provided with front entrances for the use of the lower-deck passengers and, exotically, full drop windows. Those intended for Durban also had darkened glass to cope with the fierce South African sun. They were sent to Ilford where this last attribute was not to prove so important and, during their lives, various modifications were undertaken. The diverted trolleys were, at 8ft in width, wider than normally permitted on British roads and special dispensation had to be obtained for them to run in London. This was one factor in their allocation to the remotest eastern regions of the network. After the final withdrawal of the 'SA' classes of vehicle from Ilford depot they were transferred to Poplar amidst reports in a local newspaper that they had been sold to a South American operator. These reports were denied by London Transport although the vehicles were not sold to the scrap merchant with those other vehicles withdrawn as a result of Stage Three. It was later reported that these trolleybuses were transferred to Edmonton depot. In the event, however, the remaining examples were sold to George Cohen in early 1960.

The 661 and 663 were descendants of two tram routes operated after 1910 by West Ham Corporation and the LCC — routes 61 and 63 respectively. The 661 linked Aldgate with Leyton and the 663 ran from Aldgate to Chadwell Heath. Much of the West Ham tram network had been taken over from the North Metropolitan Tramways Co, whose horse cars were replaced from 1904 onwards. A number of extensions were also constructed. Both the 61

Farewell to London's Trolleybuses

Stage... 3

18/19 August 1959

and the 63 were converted to trolleybus operation on 5 November 1939. At this time the 663 operated only as far as Ilford. Periodically there were times when it was extended to Chadwell Heath, but this extension was only made permanent on 7 January 1959 when the 695 service was withdrawn as a result of the service cuts introduced that month following the loss of traffic after the 1958 strike. This was destined to be the last 'extension' operated by London trolleybuses and was to have only a short life.

The 691 and 693 represented two short local services in Ilford. The former linked Barking Broadway with Barkingside and the latter Barking Broadway and Chadwell Heath. Both had been converted to trolleybus operation on 6 February 1938. Both routes had originally been Ilford Corporation tram routes and dated back originally to 1903. Neither route had been numbered before the creation of the LPTB. Despite the opposition of Ilford — for whom the trams had been a highly profitable enterprise — the small network passed to the LPTB in 1933. In 1934 under the rationalisation of route numbers the Barkingside service became route No 91 and that to Chadwell Heath No 93. Work started on the conversion of Ilford depot for trolleybus operation in 1937. The services were originally operated by 'E1s', but wartime vehicle shortages saw 18 Bournemouth Sunbeams transferred to Ilford in 1940. The last of these

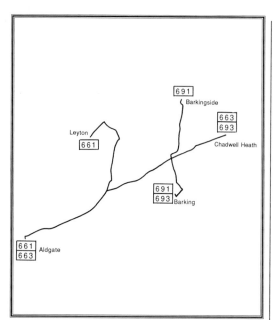

returned to Bournemouth in late 1942, by which date the vehicles originally destined for South Africa had arrived. There was also for a short period a route No 692, from Newbury Park to Chadwell Heath, but this lasted barely a year and was withdrawn in 1939. Originally it had been intended that the Ilford routes would form the final part of the conversion programme, but in the event the abandonment of these two routes was accelerated to form part of Stage Three.

Below:
'SA3' No 1748, an AEC intended for Johannesburg, speeds through Barkingside in September 1955. At one time it had been intended to leave the replacement of the relatively modern Ilford trolleybuses until much later, but there had been a steady decline in patronage, some of the class had already been withdrawn and the remainder were sent off to Colindale for breaking up.

Route Nos	Terminals	Replacement route	Type of Vehicle	Remarks
661	Aldgate-Leyton	26	RTL	32 introduced
663	Aldgate-Chadwell Heath	169A	RT	
691	Barking-Barkingside	169	RT	
693	Barking-Chadwell Heath	193	RT	

The following bus routes were amended: 25, 86

Right:
The 'N1s' were chiefly used by Bow depot on the trunk routes into central London. Here No 1588 stands outside Lea Bridge depot, the terminus of the 661, before setting off back to Aldgate. The 90 'N1s', which were AECs with Birmingham Railway & Carriage Co bodywork, were built over a 12-month period commencing in June 1939. They were the truest Cockneys of all, with the entire class being sent to Bow for the 661 and 663 routes. They were very similar to the 'J3' class, but had certain refinements which made them look rather more modern, notably the sidelights built into the front panel, radiused lower corners to the windows and, most noticeable of all, the front rainshield was swept down into the corner pillars. Produced concurrently with the Park Royal-bodied 'N2s', these were the last standard AEC trolleybuses built for London Transport. Leslie Sandler

Above:
The 691 between Barking and Barkingside was replaced by the 169. Although altered, it still links Ilford and Barkingside. Like so many suburban routes it is today operated by single-deckers. DA25, one of the handsome Optare-Delta-bodied DAFs, pulls away from a wet Ilford on 29 December 1993. Painted in a striking red and silver livery, the Deltas have a capacity almost equal to the standard London trolleybus — 40 seated and 31 standing as against 70 seated.

Left:
The one new trolleybus replacement route for Stage Three which worked into the West End was the 32. RTL244 was one of 16 allocated to Bow garage and is seen here heading down Bond Street — a thoroughfare far removed from many of the East End streets with which the trolleybuses had been familiar — on a warm June afternoon in 1960.

Left:

Aldgate pictured on 21 March 1959. Camberwell's RTL32, of the original 1948-built batch, stands beside Poplar's 'L3' trolleybus No 1490 on the 567 with a Bow 'N1' on the 661 behind it. With Bow's closure, most of the 'N1s' migrated northwestwards to Stonebridge and Colindale.

Left:

The trunk trolleybus routes from east London into the City were in several cases already duplicated for a large part of their mileage by existing motorbus services. The 10 was one example, but the chief beneficiary was the 25, where 14 additional RTs were allocated to Bow garage to cover a good part of the 663. In this scene in the Mile End Road, a bus on service 25 noses ahead, its number obscured by an Austin Cambridge and a Ford Transit, whilst RT744 on the 10 takes the inside lane. Both are bound for Victoria. This photograph dates from the late 1960s.

Left:

Contemporary with the conversion of the Bow depot routes is this photograph of RT1177, with its recently-overhauled Saunders roof-box body, loading up at Victoria.

At last we come to the Routemasters. In the late 1950s the British bus industry appeared incapable of delivering new vehicles on time, thus going a good way to preparing for its own virtual demise three decades later and, although production Routemasters had been promised for delivery in 1958, the first did not arrive until May 1959. RM8 had appeared at the Commercial Motor Show at Earl's Court in late September 1958, but this had been a one-off, being produced months before the flow-line production got started. The production line began to deliver the goods in May 1959 and the buses were allocated on trial to a number of garages which operated routes through central London. These initial RM appearances were the prelude to their mass migration to Poplar and West Ham depots where 73 of the type were required to inaugurate the fourth stage of the trolleybus replacement programme on 10/11 November 1959.

Three routes disappeared at this stage — Nos 567, 569 and 665. Poplar depot lost all its trolleybuses but some would remain at West Ham until the completion of Stage Five. Many of the vehicles affected were the most modern in the fleet — apart from the postwar 'Q1s' — and these were despatched to Finchley and Stonebridge for further service. This resulted in older vehicles being displaced and withdrawn. A total of 67 trolleybuses were taken out of service as a consequence of Stage Four. The withdrawals included the remaining 'C' class vehicles, from Stonebridge and Colindale depots. Trolleybuses were now disappearing fast from the East End and the wires came down along the Commercial Road.

Under Stage Four of the programme, all of the 'J1' trolleybuses were taken out of service, although eight were later returned to duty (Nos 908/10/14-16/20/22/25) at four different depots. Also withdrawn at this stage was the last of the 'spatted' 'C' class — No 314 from Finchley — and the last of those vehicles rebodied

Farewell to London's Trolleybuses

Stage... 4

10/11 November 1959

during the War by Weymann — No 1587A.

The routes affected by this stage were those that had featured as the last tram to trolleybus conversions in London. The 567 and the 665 were both introduced on 9 June 1940. The routes represented replacements of the 65 and 67 tram services. There was also a service 565, which represented a peak hours only service from East Ham town hall to Holborn Circus. This route, then running from Barking to Holborn and operated from Poplar, West Ham and Colindale depots, was eventually to be withdrawn on 16 October 1956. The 569, from Aldgate to Silvertown station, was introduced on 23 July 1941 as a replacement for bus route No 106. It represented a peak hours service and was extended to North Woolwich on 29 October 1941.

With the final conversions from tram to trolleybus complete, the whole programme had cost some £12 million. It is interesting to compare this cost with the £10 million that it cost to replace the trolleybuses with buses two decades later.

Route Nos	Terminals	Replacement route	Type of Vehicle	Remarks
567	Smithfield-Barking	5	RM	238 introduced
569	Aldgate-North Woolwich	48	RM	
665	Bloomsbury-Barking	5, 284	RM	

The following bus routes were amended: 9, 15, 23, 23B, 40, 169, 193

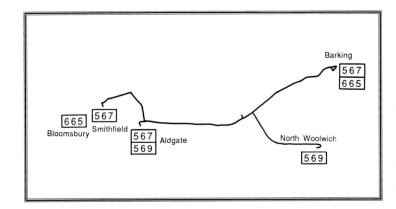

Below:
Another 'L3', this time on the 569, heads away from the docks over the long, spectacular reinforced-concrete viaduct at Silvertown Way. The viaduct is deserted apart from the trolleybus and a Ford 8 heading in the opposite direction.
Lens of Sutton

Bottom left:

*'L3' No 1476 on the 567 heads along West India Dock Road
on its way to Aldgate, with an 'N1' following partly hidden
by the road works. The cobbles marking the former tram lines
are plain to see. The 'L3s' were amongst the best-known —
and most advanced — of London's trolleybuses. A total of
150 of the type were built between August 1939 and June
1940. Long associated with east London, they spent most of
their lives based at Poplar and West Ham depots, as well as
Holloway, although many of them ended their careers
elsewhere. They were chassisless vehicles, using AEC
running units and Metro-Cammell Weymann all-metal
bodies. This form of construction stood up to service well,
receiving a severe testing over the East End's cobbles,
helping to explain the type's longevity. The curvaceous
upper-deck 'eyebrows' gave these vehicles a distinctive and
very modern appearance.* Lens of Sutton*

Above:

*Thirty-four years later an East London Titan on trolleybus
replacement service 69 is seen at the same spot, but heading
in the opposite direction towards North Woolwich. Apart
from a few more cars, the scene looks deceptively unchanged,
even down to some of the trolley standards still supporting
street-lights.*

Right:

*The 665 was directly replaced by route 5. Here RM201, on a
short working to Plaistow, stands in the forecourt of West
Ham garage. At this date, 5 April 1960, West Ham had still
(just) an allocation of trolleybuses (it was to close to
trolleybuses later that month). The vehicle behind RM201 is
none other than the pioneer RM1. It had been licensed as a
training vehicle on 10 December 1959 and would never
again carry fare-paying passengers. It served as a trainer
until 1972 when it was withdrawn and eventually preserved.
In this photograph it is carrying the radiator grille it was
supplied with in March 1957. It was given the standard, more
attractive, RM front-end assembly in February 1964.*

Above:
Another new route, replacing the whole of the 569 and the 567/665 along the Commercial Road, was the 48. This ran from North Woolwich beyond the trolleybuses' terminus at Aldgate, through the City of London, across Ludgate Circus, up Fleet Street, along the Strand and over Waterloo Bridge to the Waterloo bus terminus. Two Routemasters, RM29 and 128, are seen at Waterloo in the company of Hackney's RTW143 on 9 February 1960.

Below:
The existing 23 route between Marylebone and Becontree Heath was strengthened and operated on weekdays by nine RMs from Poplar and 36 RTs from Barking. RM1332 is pictured in Barking during March 1979. The present-day route 23, which operates from Liverpool Street to Westbourne Park, bears no resemblance to this east London route — other than being operated by Routemasters.

This stage was to see the conversion of five services operated from West Ham and Walthamstow depots. The plan envisaged the withdrawal of 34 vehicles from Walthamstow and 80 from West Ham. It was expected that this stage would also see the final withdrawal of the 'E' class trolleybuses, whilst West Ham's 'L' class vehicles were to be transferred to Finchley and Highgate depots.

The first of the routes affected by this stage was another of those that ran over the route of an ex-Leyton Corporation tram service. On 6 June 1937 the Liverpool Street-Chingford tram route No 57 was curtailed to operate between Liverpool Street and Leyton alone whilst new trolleybus service No 687 linked Leyton with Chingford Mount. The Liverpool Street-Leyton (-Chingford Mount) route was converted to trolleybus operation on 11 June 1939 as trolleybus service No 557 and the 687 was withdrawn. This conversion restored the through service that had been lost two years earlier. Through services to Chingford Mount over the metals of the LCC, Leyton and Walthamstow corporations had been introduced in 1910 and the service number 57 allocated in 1913. In March 1914 the London terminus had been moved from Moorgate to Liverpool Street. The 557 was

Below:
Stage Five of the trolleybus replacement programme took effect in April, removing West Ham's remaining trolleybuses and starting to affect those based at Walthamstow. Five routes were to be affected by this stage. West Ham-based 'L3' No 1390 pauses in the sun at Stratford Broadway, one of the great assembly points of London trolleybuses, in the company of Bow-based 'N1' No 1631 on route 661, a service which was withdrawn in August 1959. Lens of Sutton

operated from Walthamstow depot throughout its career.

The 669 linking Stratford Broadway with North Woolwich was converted to trolleybus operation in two stages. On 6 June 1937 tram route No 69, which was originally West Ham tram route No 6, from Stratford Broadway to Canning Town was converted. This route was extended from Canning Town to North Woolwich on 6 February 1938. This extension was the longest of any trolleybus deviation from the original tramway route replaced.

The 685 had its origins in a short tram route operated by Walthamstow UDC which linked Higham Hill with Markhouse Road. This route had formed one of the first stretches of Walthamstow's electric tramway when it opened on 3 June 1904. It became route No 5 when route numbers were allocated in 1928 and No 85 in 1934. When converted to trolleybus operation on 17 January 1937 the original tram route was extended at both ends: over Billet Road to the Crooked Billet, Walthamstow; and over Church Road to Lea Bridge Road. At this stage it was operated by Walthamstow depot, but on its further extension to Canning Town, as a replacement for tram route No 95, on 12 September 1937 West Ham depot assumed primary responsibility. The service was also later extended to North Woolwich.

The 689 and 690 were two short local routes in East Ham that had their origins in tram routes from Stratford Broadway to East Ham town hall and to Upton Park — routes 1 and 1A respectively. With the conversion of the routes the opportunity was taken to extend the trolleybuses over Barking Road between the two termini, thus forming a circular service. The 689 was the first to be introduced, on 12 September 1937 and operated over the circular in an anticlockwise direction. The bulk of the tram routes replaced had been inherited by the LPTB from West Ham Corporation; ironically, West Ham itself had been an early experimenter with trolleybuses, testing a Cedes-Stoll vehicle in 1912.

Route Nos	Terminals	Replacement route	Type of Vehicle	Remarks
557	Liverpool Street-Chingford Mount	257	RM	256 introduced
669	Stratford-North Woolwich	69	RM	
685	Walthamstow-North Woolwich	58	RM	
689}	Stratford-East Ham-Stratford	162}	RM, RT	
690}		272}		

Below left:
Nothing perhaps to remind us of trolleybuses at Stratford in December 1993 in the Metrobus of Grey-Green (weren't they a coach company?) on route 473 (and weren't 400-series routes supposed to be country area services?). Route 473 did not exist until 1992. The Metrobus is heading towards North Woolwich, but there is a relic from the past in the street name.

Below:
Woolwich had lost its trolleybuses in March 1959. Now the last route serving North Woolwich, on the opposite bank of the river, the 669, was to go during Stage Five. Prior to its conversion, an 'L3' waits to negotiate the turning loop, whilst another, having achieved the manoeuvre, stands ahead of an RT on route 101, pausing to pick up passengers emerging from the round, brick building beside it. This is the entrance to the Thames foot tunnel. The tall, twin funnels of one of the steam-powered Free Ferries, which linked Woolwich and North Woolwich and now long-replaced by modern diesels, can be seen behind the 'L3' facing us. Lens of Sutton

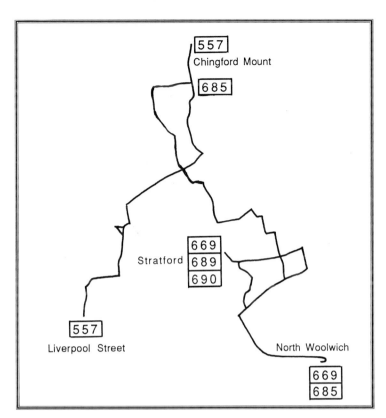

Left:
North Woolwich, still easily recognisable on 29 December 1993, sees Titans operating both the 101 and the trolleybus replacement route 669, whilst — quite inconceivable in 1959 — a Grey-Green Metrobus working on the 473 pokes its nose into the picture.

Centre left:
Bus route 69 replaced the 669. Leyland Titans are the nearest thing, apart from the seemingly indestructible Routemaster, to a purpose-designed bus still operating with London Transport. The prototype Titans entered service in 1975 and 1,125 production vehicles arrived between August 1978 and November 1984. Chiefly associated with east London, they took over many former trolleybus routes from the Routemasters. Withdrawal of the type began in 1992, but they were still dominating the east London scene when this photograph was taken of one heading down Silvertown Road towards North Woolwich at the end of December 1993. Reminders of days long gone feature in the handsome St Mary's parish church, the partly-dismantled track whence freight trains have vanished these many years leaving the now-electrified single track for passenger trains operating between North Woolwich and the North London line via Stratford, a disused semaphore bracket, a redundant reinforced-concrete arched bridge and, somewhat remarkably, a disused trolleybus overhead traction column.

Lower left:
The trolley poles of No 639, an 'E3' which spent all its career at West Ham, receive expert attention at Stratford on 17 January 1954. The bodywork of the 25 'E3s' was supplied by Park Royal, but did not last as well as some of the other classes and, as a result, withdrawals began in March 1955. Nevertheless, No 639 achieved a creditable 19.5 years in service, being amongst the final batch of the type withdrawn in October 1956. Lens of Sutton

S tage Six followed a little more than two months after Stage Five on 26 April. It was particularly extensive, removing much of what remained of the trolleybus network in east and northeast London. Twenty-three route miles of overhead disappeared, as did five routes — Nos 623, 625, 687, 697 and 699 — and a total of 104 trolleybuses. Two depots — West Ham and Walthamstow — were also to lose the last of their allocations to become diesel garages alone. The east London routes were amongst the first casualties because, with their manually-operated electrical substations, it was believed that they were amongst the more expensive services to operate.

The 623 was the oldest trolleybus service in north and east London, being converted from former tram route No 23 on 19 October 1936. Originally operated by Walthamstow Corporation until 1933, the replacement trolleybus route had been extended beyond the original tram terminus over the River Lea to a new destination at Manor House. Introduced on 8 May 1938, the 625 was also a route that ran over part of the ex-23 tram service, but instead of serving Manor House underground station, it ran to Wood Green. The 623 and 625 services were

Below:
One of West Ham's routes to survive until Stage Six was the 699 from the Victoria and Albert Docks to Chingford Mount. Here 'L3' No 1405 speeds past a Routemaster inside the depot on 5 April 1960. The posters either side of the route indicator are somewhat ironic; there were only a very few weeks left for anyone to drive or conduct a 699.

integrated and at peak periods the 625 trolleybuses were extended to Winchmore Hill. Both the 623 and 625 were operated by Walthamstow depot, although Wood Green contributed a small number for the 625 during peak hours only.

Operated by West Ham depot, the 687 replaced the former 87 tram route on 6 June 1937. The service had been cut back from Chingford Mount to Walthamstow on 11 June 1939 with the introduction of the 557, whilst in July 1942 it was diverted away from Leyton High Road to run over Church Road, Markhouse Road and Blackhorse Road. The 697 and 699 — converted to trolleybus operation on 6 June 1937 — both linked Chingford Mount with the Victoria & Albert Docks and both were operated

by vehicles from Walthamstow and West Ham depots. The 697, originally LPTB tram route No 97, was inherited from Walthamstow and West Ham corporations. The 699 had its origins in a second tram service from the Docks which West Ham inaugurated in 1912 to relieve congestion on the main Docks service. It became service 99 in 1933, whilst a short working, route No 99A, was to remain tram operated until March 1938.

The last trolleybus to enter West Ham depot, on 26 April 1960, was No 622 on service 699, which was suitably decorated for the occasion. This vehicle had been retained when the remainder of the class had been withdrawn as No 622 had also inaugurated trolleybus operation in the area.

Route Nos	Terminals	Replacement route	Type of Vehicle	Remarks
623	Manor House-Woodford	123	RM, RTW	
625	Winchmore Hill-Woodford	275	RM	
687	Walthamstow-Victoria & Albert Docks	278	RM	
697	Chingford Mount-Victoria & Albert Docks	249A	RM	
699	Chingford Mount-Victoria & Albert Docks	249	RM	299 introduced
The following bus routes were amended: 34, 41, 69				

Below left:
Amongst the replacement services worked by new Routemasters was the 256, which covered, in part, both the 557 and the 685, and ran from Moorgate to Chingford Mount. RM163 of Walthamstow stands at its Moorgate terminus on 5 April 1960, whilst No 829, a March 1938-built 'H1' trolleybus with a chassis by Leyland and fitted with MCW bodywork, stands alongside. No 829 spent its entire career at Wood Green and, in February 1961, was the very last member of its class to be withdrawn. Amongst the trolleybuses withdrawn as a result of Stage Five were all the remaining 'E1s' and 'E2s' with the exception of No 622. The reason for this vehicle's survival will shortly be revealed.

Below:
Both the 256 and 257, although altered, still exist. Capital Citybus have been operating the 257, which runs from Stratford to Chingford, since the summer of 1992. An East Lancashire-bodied Dennis Dominator stands at Stratford, about to operate a short working to Walthamstow on 29 December 1993.

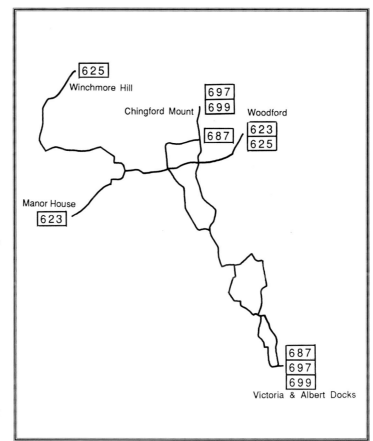

Left:

No 902, an 'H1' trolleybus based at Walthamstow, is pursued by an Eastern National Bristol Lodekka whilst working on the 625 between Wood Green and Woodford. A total of 150 'H1s' were built between February and October 1938 and the type was based at a number of depots dotted around the system. Three were destroyed during the war, the rest were withdrawn between September 1955 and February 1961. A. D. Packer

Below left:

'J1' No 936 of Walthamstow depot pulls up to let the gentleman in the long brown macintosh alight at Custom House station beside the Royal Victoria Docks in January 1960, some three months before the 637 disappeared. There were 48 'J1s', AEC chassis with Weymann bodywork, constructed. No 936 was delivered in March 1938 and was withdrawn a few days after this picture was taken. It spent almost its entire career working out of Finchley depot, only being transferred to Walthamstow for the final few months.
Michael Dryhurst

Above right:

'K1' No 1272, also of Walthamstow depot, heads west along Ferry Road — I wonder when anyone last travelled by ferry in Walthamstow? — working the 623 from Woodford to Manor House in April 1956. With the closure of Walthamstow, No 1272 moved to Wood Green from where it was withdrawn in April 1961.

Centre right:

'C3' No 333 of Walthamstow and 'K1' No 1099 of Stamford Hill stand at Wood Green in the early 1950s. No 333, a BRCW-bodied AEC built in August 1936, was withdrawn in May 1955, well before the trolleybus replacement programme started, and was broken up by Birds at Stratford-upon-Avon a year later. No 1099, an all-Leyland vehicle built in December 1938, would last exactly six years longer. V. C. Jones/IAL

Lower right:

'E2' class No 622 inaugurated trolleybus operation from West Ham with some ceremony in June 1936. With the end of electric traction looming this fact was remembered and the depot refused to let No 622 head for the scrapyard with the remainder of the class in February 1960. It became, with equal ceremony, the depot's last trolleybus and is seen here on the wet and gloomy last afternoon — 26 April 1960. Three months later it made its last journey to the scrapyard at Colindale. Lens of Sutton

Left:
Stage Seven, on 20 July 1960, saw the abandonment of London's most famous trolleybus destination — 'Nr Willesden Junction'. To be strictly correct this destination had actually begun to be replaced by the more prosaic 'Harlesden College Park' a short while earlier. No 452 illustrates the earlier destination at West Croydon in September 1954. No 452 belonged to the 'D2' class and was one of 99 MCW-bodied Leylands built between October 1936 and May 1937. This class was associated with Hammersmith depot for over 20 years. This example was amongst the last of the class to be withdrawn, succumbing in April 1959.

Right:
Each Christmas Day — and we're talking about the times, long past, when you could travel by public transport on Christmas Day itself — Carshalton depot operated a short working of the 630 from West Croydon to Mitcham. Here one of the second batch of 'B1s', No 492, stands at West Croydon on Christmas Day 1958.
Lens of Sutton

Left:
No 743 poses at the same location on 29 June 1960 showing the adoption of the new destination. This was an all-Leyland 'F1' class and was built in November 1937. No 743 spent most of its career, like the rest of the 100-strong class, at Hanwell, but was transferred for the last year or so to Hammersmith where it replaced a 'D' class vehicle. No 743 was, in November 1960, also amongst the final batch of its class to be withdrawn.

This stage marked the halfway point in the trolleybus conversion programme and saw four routes converted to diesel bus operation. These abandonments meant the end of trolleybus operation out of Hammersmith depot and the loss of one service from Highgate.

The routes affected had had an interesting and varied history. The 611, introduced on 10 December 1939, served Highgate Village. This route was renowned for the steepness of Highgate Hill and this aspect played an important part in the route's history. The section up Highgate Hill was originally operated by a 3ft 6in gauge cable tramway which, when it opened in 1884, was the first cable tramway in Europe. Although having a chequered history, the cable service was to remain until 1909; it was replaced by electric trams the following year. A number of the 'J3' and 'L1' trolleybuses were fitted with run-back brakes to ensure safe operation over the 611 route.

The 626 was introduced on 12 September 1937 and was based largely on ex-LCC tram route No 26 and ex-LUT service 89. It was a weekday peak hour service linking Acton with Clapham; the rump of LCC route No 26 was to disappear in September 1950 as part of Operation Tramaway. Another service to operate to Clapham Junction was the 628 which originated as part of LCC tram route No 28 and was converted to trolleybus operation on 12 September 1937. Although at the time of conversion both the 626 and 628 were

Farewell to London's Trolleybuses
Stage... 7
19/20 July 1960

Below:
The Hammersmith-operated routes should originally have been amongst the last to be converted but various factors, chiefly the construction of Hammersmith flyover (which would have meant expensive new overhead) and the wish to use the trolleybus depot as the base for BEA's fleet of RF airport coaches, brought about their premature demise. By the end more modern vehicles — 'K1s' and 'K2s' as well as the older 'F1s' — had replaced all the original 'D' class vehicles. On the last day, 19 July 1960, 'K1' No 1125 breasts the summit of Pitlake Bridge — below which run the Southern electric lines from West Croydon to Wimbledon, Sutton and Epsom Downs — its long journey almost over, in more ways than one.

Left:

A Cohen's 600 Group Scammell sets off from Hammersmith depot on 8 July 1960 towing a 'K1' on its last journey to the scrapyard behind Colindale depot. The 'K2' behind it, No 1240, lasted only a little longer, making the same journey later that month. To its right is a breakdown tender converted from an STL bus.

Centre left:

Two other Hammersmith-operated routes disappeared at this time. These were the 626 from Acton to Clapham Junction and the 628 from Craven Park to Clapham Junction. 'D2' trolleybus No 439 is pictured at Clapham Junction on the 628 with 'E/1' class tram No 775 on the 26 in 1938. Author's Collection

Below left:

Clapham Junction is seen on 30 August 1991, 53 years later. Three Metrobuses are seen: one on the long-established 37 from Peckham to Putney, one on the more recent 295 from Ladbroke Grove to Clapham Junction, and the third on the 77a from Wandsworth to the Aldwych.

Below:

'P1' No 1721 begins its journey from East Croydon to Harlesden on 5 March 1959. No 1721 was the very last prewar-designed trolleybus to enter service, appearing in October 1941. There were 25 of these handsome MCW-bodied Leylands. They were very similar in appearance to the 'L3s', but were of conventional construction with a separate chassis and were, consequently, slightly taller. For a numerically small class the 'P1s' were well travelled. No 1721 was withdrawn when Hammersmith depot closed. The 630 was London's longest all-day trolleybus service, running a distance of some 14.5 miles. I never quite travelled the whole distance — a single journey took 77min — usually alighting a few hundred yards short, within sight of the terminus, at the big girder bridge which carried Scrubs Lane over the Western Region main line out of Paddington.

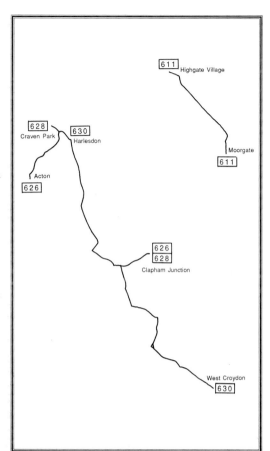

operated by Hammersmith depot, this arrangement had only been in force since the service reductions of January 1959; prior to that date Stonebridge had housed the vehicles used on both services.

At more than 14 miles in length, the 630 from Harlesden to West Croydon was the longest of all London's trolleybus routes. It had been converted to trolleybus operation on 12 September 1937.

Below:
It was at this location that the author used to sit and watch 'Kings', 'Castles' and the other Western Region steam classes; a location where, every now and again, the deep hoot of a Stanier whistle from nearby Willesden Junction would interrupt the Swindon idyll. I never managed to get a trolleybus and train to coincide so I trust that you will be content with this picture of the traction standards above the chimney of 'Castle' class No 5067 Isambard Kingdom Brunel as the locomotive speeds towards Paddington with a 13-coach excursion train from South Wales on 22 March 1959.

Route Nos	Terminals	Replacement route	Type of Vehicle	Remarks
611	Moorgate-Highgate Village	271	RM	
626	Acton-Clapham Junction}	268	RM	
628	Craven Park-Clapham Junction}			
630	Harlesden-West Croydon	220	RM	

The following bus routes were amended: 64, 71

Above:
A route quite unrelated to the Hammersmith ones was also converted as a result of Stage Seven. This was the 611 from Moorgate to Highgate Village. No 1048, a Highgate-allocated 'J3' — an AEC dating from October 1938 fitted with BRCW bodywork and complete with run-back brakes to prevent any unfortunate occurrences on Highgate Hill — charges the foothills prior to assaulting the summit in July 1960 a few days before both route and vehicle disappeared. The wide open windows of both trolleybuses would suggest a steaming hot day; the attire of the pedestrians indicates something quite different. Very puzzling. Michael Dryhurst

Left:
The 220 achieved fame by becoming the very first route, along with the tram replacement route 95, to operates DMSs — 'Londoners' as they were officially known, although this was soon forgotten. DMS1 poses at Park Royal, shortly after completion, before entering service on Saturday 2 January 1971. It is now preserved by London Transport.
London Transport

Below:
'Feltham' No 353, in its original LUT livery at Ealing Broadway, makes the S-type bus alongside look like something from prehistory. Author's Collection

Left:
This was the scene in West Croydon on the first day of Routemaster operation in the town on 20 July 1960. The replacement of the 630 was the 220, which was operated by 37 RMs from Shepherds Bush (40 on Saturdays and 25 on Sundays). The 64, which had previously been involved in the 654 replacement, now also figured in that of the 630, being extended from West Croydon to Wimbledon Stadium. Elmers End was allocated seven Routemasters (Monday-Saturday) and four on Sundays, for this duty. A new registration series, WLT, featured on the Routemasters for these replacement services. RM270, VLT270, heads off home to Elmers End whilst Shepherds Bush-allocated RM369, WLT369, waits to return to Scrubs Lane.

Above:
'F1' No 680 is pictured on its way to Clapham Junction on route 655. Michael Rooum

Below:
A well-loaded 'F1', No 692, passes Southall bus garage on its way to Uxbridge in November 1955. Behind the wall on the right is the AEC works. Stage Eight brought about the end of the 'F1s'.

This stage removed London trolleybuses from their westernmost outpost — Uxbridge. The long 607 from Shepherds Bush to Uxbridge, together with the 655 from Hanwell to Hammersmith — extended to Clapham Junction in rush hours — were both worked from Hanwell depot. Hanwell was always associated with the 100-strong 'F1' class, which were all-Leyland vehicles built between March and December 1937. These had taken over from those most splendid of tramcars, the 'Felthams', which had then moved on to pastures new — not that there were many pastures in Brixton and Streatham where they later lived, or indeed in Leeds where they migrated when their service in London was over. These were also the first conversions to affect routes inherited by the LPTB from the London United Tramways.

The 607 had a long history. Its origins lay in a horse tramway opened in 1876 from Shepherds Bush to Acton Lane. The line passed eventually to the London United Tramways in 1894. Although the electrification of the line proceeded well and was completed for an opening in 1900, this was delayed until 4 April 1901 (the formal opening taking place on 10 July 1901 — the first

Below:
London's last trolleybuses, the LYH-registered 'Q1s', were delivered between May and December 1952. A number of the class were based at Hanwell to operate the 607. The very last of all, No 1891, is seen here on an enthusiasts' tour at the Uxbridge terminus of the 607. Lens of Sutton

electric tramway opened in London) whilst the LUT helped fund the transfer of the Kew Observatory to Teddington — there were fears that the electric trams would interfere with the observatory's scientific equipment. The route was converted to trolleybus operation on 15 November 1936.

The other conversion at this stage, the 655, was also part of the London United Tramways network; indeed, it was the last ex-LUT route converted to trolleybus operation. The conversion to trolleybus operation took place on 13 December 1936.

Although latterly served by Hanwell depot, both services were operated for a short period in the 1930s from vehicles based at Acton. This depot had been converted to trolleybus operation in 1936 primarily to serve routes 660 and 666, but it was not to remain operational for long, being closed at the end of the same year.

Below:
The 607 was replaced by the 207 bus route. DMS1164 is seen on this service in Uxbridge during 1979.

Route Nos	Terminals	Replacement route	Type of Vehicle	Remarks
607	Shepherds Bush-Uxbridge	207	RM	207A introduced
655	Acton Vale-Clapham Junction	255	RM	

The following bus route were amended: 120

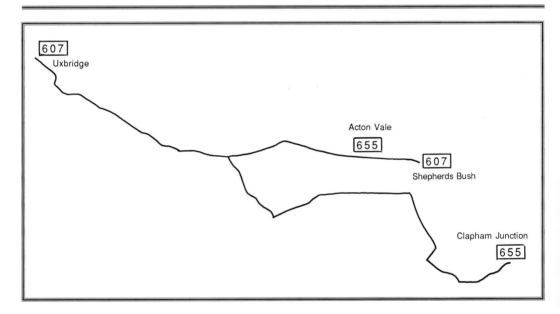

During the course of 1961 the London trolleybus was brought perilously close to extinction. Four stages in the conversion programme took place between the end of January and 8 November, which meant that by Christmas there remained only two stages to go. Stage Nine affected seven routes, with a total mileage of 51 route miles. All the services were operated from Highgate depot. This depot had originally been known as Holloway, gaining its new name of Highgate in 1951 when operations were merged with Central Area bus services.

Routes 513 and 613, which had their origins in a horse tramway built in the 1870s connecting King's Cross with Camden with subsequent extensions that were later converted by the LCC into an electric tramway, both linked Hampstead Heath with Parliament Hill Fields via Holborn Circus. The route of the 613 was identical to that of the 513 but operated in the reverse direction. Both services, operated from Highgate depot, were converted to trolleybus operation on 10 July 1938. The 517 and 617, linking North Finchley and Holborn, were also operated as reverse routes. Again the route originated as a horse tramway constructed in the 1870s. During the 1880s the route had been the scene of an experiment in the use of compressed air trams.

Farewell to London's Trolleybuses

Stage... 9

31 January/1 February 1961

Below:
The largest depot of all, Holloway, lost all but 22 of its 127 trolleybuses on 1 February. Until less than a decade earlier the depot had housed trams, trolleybuses and motorbuses. This scene, taken on 5 April 1952, shows two 'E/3' trams, Nos 199 and 195, about to make a last journey through the Kingsway subway, standing between replacement RT3481 and a 1935 Ford 8, whilst just visible on the far left is a row of trolleybuses. V. C. Jones/IAL

The routes had been converted to trolleybus operation on 6 March 1938. The 617 ceased to operate on Sundays after March 1954, whilst the 517 was cut back from Holborn to King's Cross on Sundays from the same date. Prior to 1941 Finchley had provided a number of vehicles to supplement those from Highgate in use on the service.

The 615, also converted to trolleybus operation on 10 July 1938, was the heir to ex-LCC tram route No 15. This had its origins in a horse tram route introduced in June 1871, with further developments taking place until electric cars were introduced to Parliament Hill Fields in 1911. The other two routes to succumb at this stage also had a long history. The 639 dated back to a London Street Tramways route opened in 1887 that became an LCC electric tram route in 1909. It was converted to trolleybus operation on 10 July 1939. Finally, the 653 developed from a network of horse tram routes constructed by the North Metropolitan Co from 1871 onwards. Electrified by the LCC, the resulting trolleybus route, converted on 5 March 1939, was one of the longest in London. It had originally been proposed to extend this, and two other routes, further down Tottenham Court Road, but these proposals failed in the light of objections to overhead from a number of residents.

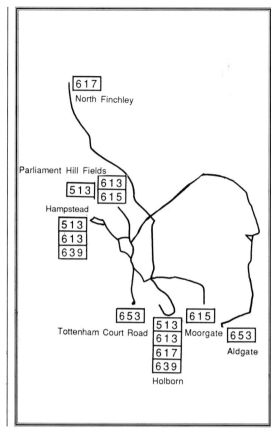

Route Nos	Terminals	Replacement route	Type of Vehicle	Remarks
513} 613}	Hampstead Heath-Holborn-Parliament Hill Fields	45, 63	RT, RTW	
615	Moorgate-Parliament Hill Fields	214	RM	
517} 617}	Holborn-North Finchley	17	RM	143 extended to cover
639	Moorgate-Hampstead Heath	239	RM	
653	Aldgate-Tottenham Court Road	253	RM	

The following bus routes were amended: 39, 143

Below left:
An 'M1' and an 'L3', both with their poles down, stand outside the depot on 9 November 1960. The leading vehicle, No 1546, belongs to a class not yet illustrated. The 25 'M1s' had lightweight AEC chassis fitted with MCW bodywork and were based on a prototype, No 953, produced in 1938. The prototype had been burned out in 1943. The class was built between November 1939 and January 1940, and worked in east London for some 15 years until gradually migrating westwards. Thereafter they were chiefly allocated to Highgate. No 1546 was withdrawn in November 1961. The 653, which ran from Aldgate to a big loop through Hackney, Stamford Hill, Manor House, Holloway and Camden Town to Tottenham Court Road, was one of seven trolleybus routes to disappear at this time.

Above right:
'L3' No 1527 bounces over the cobbles outside King's Cross station on 8 July 1960. This, one of the last batch of 'L3s' (built in June 1940), was one of five fitted with slide vent windows. It was also withdrawn in November 1961.

Right:
'L2' No 1374 is pictured at Holborn on 20 May 1960. The only difference between the 513 and 613 routes was that they operated in alternative directions around the Holborn loop. There were just nine 'L2s', which were identical to the vastly more numerous 'L3s' except that all the side windows had square corners. The 'L2s' represented an intermediate design between the all-square windows, including the front, of the earlier standard vehicles and the curved lines of later ones; although, inevitably, there were exceptions.

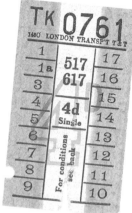

Top:

'N2' No 1652 passes the handsome King's Cross hotel on a sunny July afternoon in 1955 on its way to Hampstead Heath. This was a Park Royal-bodied AEC, delivered in November 1939. Despite being such a prolific builder of bodies for London Transport, Park Royal trolleybuses were relatively rare in the capital. Rather like the contemporary 'P1s', the 25 'N2s' had something of a wanderlust, beginning their careers in east London and all but two ending their time at Stonebridge. No 1652 was withdrawn in January 1962. In the far distance can be seen the celebrated gasworks, which still exist — indeed they are now group listed buildings — and which have appeared in countless feature films and TV programmes. Just visible in front of them are a couple of Birch Brothers double-deck coaches.

Above:

'L3' No 1380 operates the 517 along Holloway Road at the junction of Camden Road and Seven Sisters Road (better known as the Nag's Head) on 9 November 1960. The 'L3' takes the inside line whilst three representatives of the British Motor Corporation — a Wolsley 1500, a Farina A40 and an A35 — take the outer. No 1380, the first of its class, was the only trolleybus with an 'FXF' registration. Built in August 1939, it moved from Holloway to Fulwell and was amongst the final withdrawals in May 1962. To connoisseurs there was something unique about the ambience of the Nag's Head. The Gaumont, a magnificent example of an interwar art deco picture palace, contributed to it. Remarkably, the cinema, now an Odeon, still survives. The Nag's Head, just down the road from Arsenal's ground at Highbury, was the busiest junction on the entire trolleybus system — a wonderful place to watch trolleybuses clicking and hissing their way about their business. I used to love drawing the complicated knitting of the overhead and, once, leaning against the safety barrier, an Edmonton 'K1', its rear wheels rubbing the kerb, clipped the edge of my sketch book and sent the bottle of Indian ink spinning over my masterpiece.

Top right:
The Nag's Head, 35 years later, is pictured on 22 February 1994. All the buildings remain intact, the functional railings have been replaced by trendy pseudo-antique ones. Motor cars are now represented by a Japanese import and a German BMW — now, it is to be supposed, a relation of the former BMC by marriage. A brand-new Northern Counties Palatine II-bodied Volvo Olympian 210 of London Suburban heads for Moorgate on the 271. The 271 is virtually the only former trolleybus route — the 611 — completely unaltered since trolleybus days except for more modern vehicles. London Suburban registers most of its buses on Merseyside and sometimes transfers them to and from Liverpool and London. I travelled to Finsbury Square (Moorgate) on a Palatine Olympian later that day and, apart from the upstairs front grab rail precisely at eye level, found it a particularly comfortable and altogether impressive vehicle.

Above right:
Bus route 17 replaced the 517/617 trolleybus routes and was extended on across the City of London to Camberwell Green. Finchley 'L3' No 1488 takes a respectful place in the rear behind Highgate's RM575 on the latter's first day in service — 1 February 1961.

Right:
Amongst the replacement motorbus services was the 253, which replaced the former 653. RM1978 is pictured at Aldgate on this service on 19 February 1980.

Bottom right:
Trolleybus route 615 was replaced by bus service 214. More than 30 years later the route still exists and is little changed from trolleybus days beyond an extension from Moorgate to Liverpool Street and London Bridge. However, the vehicles could hardly be more different. Thamesway, part of the Bristol-based Badgerline Group — hence the badger on the side — now operates the route with Dennis Darts — Plaxton Pointer-bodied single-deckers. No 902 stands at Liverpool Street, on the site of Broad Street station, on 22 February 1994 amongst a richly varied assortment of vehicles, including an East London Titan and Renault Hoppa, a D&J Travel Leyland Lynx II working the London City Airport shuttle, and RML2664 of Westbourne garage with newly-applied Gold Arrow fleetname.

Left:
Stage Ten of the trolleybus conversion programme took place on 26 April 1961 and involved all the routes which used the West End terminus of Tottenham Court Road. 'H1' No 865 brings up the rear of a group of 'J2s' and 'K1s' in Fitzroy Street on 5 April 1960. Tottenham Court Road itself is located where the cars are congregating at the end of the street.

Above:
Four routes disappeared as a result of this stage. Edmonton's 'P1' No 1715 nips in between a Ford Consul and a mini as it turns into the Seven Sisters Road at the Nag's Head on 9 November 1960 whilst operating on the 659.

Left:
'P1' No 1711 is pictured having just turned at Smithfield on a wet May morning in 1960.

This stage of the conversion programme was to see trolleybuses withdrawn from a number of routes that served north London. A total of four services, operated from Edmonton, Highgate and Wood Green depots, were to disappear and 144 trolleybuses were to be withdrawn, including the remaining 'Q1s'. A total of 125 of the 127 'Q1s' were to be exported to Spain between January and November 1961. The two exceptions were Nos 1768, which was preserved, and 1841, which was dismantled following withdrawal in November 1960 and its motors transferred to Imperial College London.

The first of the quartet to be converted at this stage was the 627, which had its origins as LPTB tram route 27 (which linked Euston Road with Edmonton and was operated before 1933 by the LCC and MET). This particular route, being served by three depots — Wood Green, Highgate and Edmonton — was unique amongst London's trolleybus services.

The 629 originated as LPTB tram route 29 and was converted to trolleybus operation on 8 May 1938. The final extension to the tram route had seen electric trams first reach Enfield

Farewell to London's Trolleybuses
Stage... 10
25/26 April 1961

Below:
Another well-known gathering point of trolleybuses which was now much reduced was Manor House. Highgate 'L2' No 1372 heads past the impressive pile on 19 April 1961. Built in June 1939, No 1372 had, like the 627 route, just one week of service left.

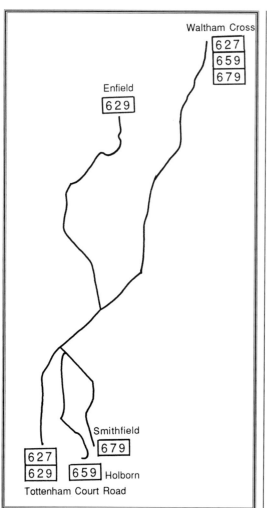

Waltham Cross

627
659
679

Enfield

629

Smithfield

679

627
629

659 Holborn

Tottenham Court Road

on 1 July 1909. The original tram route, which was largely within the MET area, was of historical significance in as much as it was the first example of through running between the MET and LCC when such services were introduced in August 1912. As a tram route it had operated in later years with the 'Felthams', before their transfer south of the river. It was operated from Wood Green depot; this depot had been constructed in 1937 on the site of an older depot. Originally the conversion of the 629 was scheduled to form part of Stage Twelve, but plans for the implementation of a one-way system along Tottenham Court Road and Gower Street required that this conversion was brought forward seven months.

Operated from Edmonton and Highgate depots — the latter during early weekday mornings only — route 679 (from Smithfield to Waltham Cross) had been converted to trolleybus operation on 16 October 1938. Its origins lay in a horse tramway, between Islington and Smithfield, operated by the LCC from 1907 and electrified the following year. A connection was made with an older horse tramway at Islington. As service No 79 it was linked with the MET service to Edmonton in 1913 and extended to Waltham Cross in 1914. Initially the trolleybuses travelled beyond Ponders End only on Sundays, but the service was extended to Waltham Cross on weekdays after 1938.

Below:
An 'L3' and two 'K1s' head past Manor House towards the West End on 19 April 1961.

Route Nos	Terminals	Replacement route	Type of Vehicle	Remarks
627	Tottenham Court Road-Waltham Cross	127	RM	276, 279A introduced
629	Tottenham Court Road-Enfield	269	RM, RT	
659	Holborn-Waltham Cross	259	RM	
679	Smithfield-Waltham Cross	279	RM	

The following bus route were amended: 29

Above:
*Enfield lost its only trolleybus route
with the withdrawal of the 629.
Based at Wood Green, the 'H1s',
built between February and October
1938, monopolised the 629 until
replaced by the 'K1s' just before
the end. An 'H1' is caught at
Enfield Cross Road.
Author's Collection*

Right:
*A long-established motorbus route
involved in the replacement of the
629 was the 29, although it would be
some time before Routemasters were
allocated to it. RM1349 stands in
Grosvenor Place.*

Below right:
*A group of no fewer than eight
trolleybuses stand outside
Edmonton depot. The nearest
vehicles, the 659 with its back to us
and the 679 facing, represent two
final two prewar classes: 'P1'
No 1715 and 'K3' No 1685. The 25
'K3s', although constructed between
October and December 1940 (more
than a year into World War 2), were
virtually identical to the 'K1s' and
'K2s'. The only visible difference
were the sidelights, which were set
into the front panels. The vehicles
were allocated to Edmonton for all
their operational career. Both
classes disappeared in the Stage
Eleven abandonment, a sure sign
that the end was nigh for all
London trolleybuses.*

Above:
Three trolleybuses on route 647, with 'K2' No 1310 on the left and 'K1' No 1130 on the right, stand amongst the warehouses at the London Docks terminus on 8 February 1961. This route, along with the 543/643, used up Stamford Hill's allocation of 48 'K1' and 'K2' vehicles. Stamford Hill also worked the Sundays Only 649A service from Liverpool Street to Wood Green which also disappeared as a result of this stage.

Below:
'K1' No 1148 is pictured on route 647 on 13 July 1961 at Leman Street, Aldgate, being led by a brewery dray.
Leslie Sandler

Amongst the routes which disappeared in Stage Eleven on 19 July 1961 was the 649 and, thus, trolleybuses would be seen no more at their northernmost extremity — Waltham Cross — a place which still retained something of a village atmosphere. Rather less village-like was the City terminus of the 649 — Liverpool Street. Another pair of Holborn routes, the 543/643 to Wood Green, also went, along with the last route to serve the Docks — the 647 — which ran between Stamford Hill and London Docks. Edmonton and Stamford Hill depots became Routemaster garages.

Introduced on 6 February 1939, the weekdays-only 543 was a conversion of tram route 43 — which had been electrified by the LCC in 1907 — and the section north of Stamford Hill on the LCC-MET route No 71. The 543 operated around the Holborn loop in an anticlockwise direction, whilst linked route No 643 traversed the loop clockwise. The 647, converted on 5 February 1939, linked London Docks with Stamford Hill. It had origins as a horse tram route in the 1870s, being converted

Farewell to London's Trolleybuses

Stage... 11
18/19 July 1961

Below:
Stamford Hill-based 'K1' No 1255 is pictured at Holborn on 20 May 1960.

by the LCC to electric traction in 1907 and becoming route No 47 in 1914. The 649, which was inaugurated on 16 October 1938, ran from Liverpool Street to Waltham Cross. Again with a history stretching back to the horse-tram era, the electric services were operated by both the MET and LCC after June 1920 when the latter's route

No 49 was extended over the former's route No 10. The 649 trolleybuses initially operated from Ponders End to Stamford Hill, but were extended to Liverpool Street in February 1939. The Sundays-only 649A dated from the early years of World War 2, but received its route number only in 1949.

Route Nos	Terminals	Replacement route	Type of Vehicle	Remarks
543}	Holborn-Wood Green	243	RM	
643}				
647	London Docks-Stamford Hill	67	RM	
649	Liverpool Street-Waltham Cross	149	RM	
649A	Liverpool Street-Wood Green (Sundays Only)	243A	RM	

The following bus route were amended: 47

Left:
It is 19 July 1961 and the last 643 is ceremoniously escorted by drivers, conductors and conductresses in Stamford Hill depot. London Transport

Above:
The 649 was replaced by the 149 which was extended to Victoria. An interesting development, nearly two decades later in 1980, was the use of former Green Line Routemaster coaches, with their doors removed, from Tottenham garage on this route. RCL2229 set off from Victoria in September that year.

Below:
Also used as a trolleybus replacement route was the 47, which was extended from Shoreditch to Stoke Newington. Catford-based RT3284 heads south through Bermondsey on its way home.

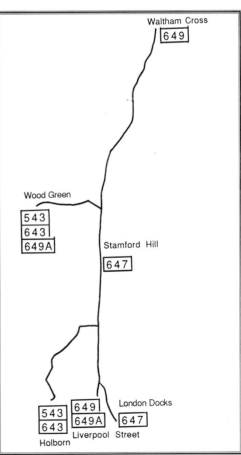

The fourth and last stage in the programme for 1961 occurred on 7 November 1961 and involved four routes: the 521 (the last route in the 5xx series) and the 621 between High Holborn and Finchley; the 609 from Barnet to Moorgate; and the 641 from Winchmore Hill to Moorgate.

The 521 and 621 — the difference was that the 621 traversed the Holborn loop in a clockwise direction whilst the 521 undertook the same manoeuvre anticlockwise — had been converted from former MET/LCC tram route 21. The MET section ran from Finsbury Park to North Finchley, whilst those of the LCC linked Holborn with Finsbury Park. As with a number of other ex-MET lines, the 21 tram route had been associated with the 'Felthams' until the route's conversion to trolleybus operation on 6 March 1938. It was served by trolleybuses based at Finchley depot.

Farewell to London's Trolleybuses

Stage... **12**

7/8 November 1961

Left:
No 954 stands at Moorgate at dusk on 11 November 1960. This was a unique vehicle, the prototype of the chassisless vehicles, and was classified 'L2'. This was remarkable as it differed in several respects from the production run and, normally, the smallest variation would result in London Transport slapping on a new designation. The most noticeable differences were the lack of curved 'eyebrows' over the upper deck front windows and the yellow line

carried under the driver's windows — the only trolleybus in the London fleet so adorned. No 954 entered service in March 1938 and was withdrawn in April 1961, being scrapped two months later. Leslie Sandler

Below:
Moorgate is pictured on 29 April 1961 with Wood Green 'K2' No 1311 on the 641 overtaking Finchley 'L3' No 1484 on the 609.

Top:
*Another non-standard vehicle is seen at Moorgate. 'H1'
No 792 was one of the unfortunate trolleybuses caught in the
bombing of Bexleyheath in November 1940. Its body was
destroyed and it is seen here with the replacement, of more
modern design with slide vent windows, built by Weymann in
November 1941. D. A. Jones; London Trolleybus Society*

Above:
*The Tally Ho!, North Finchley, was another favourite
trolleybus haunt. On 8 February 1961 'L3' No 1510, on the
521, and 'N1' No 1643, on the 660, bring up the rear of a*

*group of five. The front pair are both on route 609. Certain
detail differences between these MCW and BRCW-bodied
AECs can be detected, notably the cut-away panelling over
the platform on the 'L3' and variations in the details around
the upper deck rear windows. The Metropolitan Police
licence plate, which all trams and trolleybuses (but no
contemporary diesel buses) carried, can be seen below the
used ticket box on No 1643. No 1643, a Stonebridge vehicle,
was withdrawn in January 1962, whilst No 1510 was
transferred from Finchley, after the 521 expired, to Fulwell
and lasted until the final day of trolleybus operation in May
1962.*

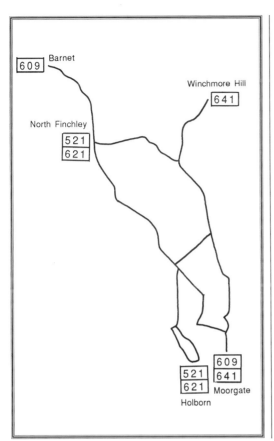

The 609, from Moorgate to Barnet, was operated by trolleybuses from both Finchley and Highgate — the latter on Sundays only. Again introduced on 6 March 1938, the new trolleybus service replaced trams on route 9 (Moorgate-North Finchley) and on the northern section of route 19 (to Barnet). The conversion of the 609 was unique in as much as during the last six months of trolleybus operation Sunday services were operated by a combination of trolleybuses and replacement Routemaster buses.

The 641, linking Moorgate with Winchmore Hill, was throughout its operational career, linked with the 629. However, as already noted, the 629 was converted in Stage Ten as a result of traffic requirements. This left the 641 to operate alone up the former MET tram route to Winchmore Hill. The trolleybus service had been introduced on 8 May 1938 and was a replacement for tram route No 41.

Below:
Finchley depot pictured on 8 November 1961. From left to right we see RML888, a breakdown tender converted from a prewar STL and 'L3' No 1460. The trolleybus, still displaying its 621 route blinds from its last journey the previous evening, should have departed with its brothers during the small hours of the morning but, presumably, a fault brought about a stay of execution. Some 'L3s' remained at Finchley after this date to work the 645.

Route Nos	Terminals	Replacement route	Type of Vehicle	Remarks
521}	Holborn-North Finchley	221	RM	168A extended to cover, 4A introduced
621}				
609	Moorgate-Barnet	104	RM, RML	
641	Moorgate-Winchmore Hill	141	RM	

The following bus routes were amended: 48, 168, 179

Top:
Without doubt the most exciting aspect of the 609 replacement (unless you were a trolleybus) was the appearance of that still-familiar London vehicle, the RML. The first 15 of these lengthened 72-seat Routemasters were allocated to Finchley to work the 104, a service which took over from the 609. RML894, on its first day in service, and 'L3' No 1449, on the 645, meet at Finchley on 8 November 1961. It was on this day that lower-case lettering for the destination blinds first appeared in London.

Above:
Colindale's 'C2' No 201 heads for Canons Park, a location which was very nearly out in the country. No 201 had been delivered in 1936 and was to remain in service until September 1955. It went to Stratford-upon-Avon early the following year for scrap. V. C. Jones/IAL

And so we come to 1962, the final year of trolleybus operation in London. On 1 January 200 vehicles were scheduled to operate on 11 routes. Hardly had the New Year dawned than this was whittled down to a little over 90 vehicles for seven routes. On 2 January four routes — the 645 from Canons Park to Barnet, the 660 North Finchley-Hammersmith, the 662 Sudbury-Paddington Green and the 666 from Edgware to Hammersmith — were withdrawn. Finchley and Stonebridge depots went over to diesel bus operation and Colindale depot closed. The unique 'C2s' with spats over the rear wheels were particularly associated with the Stonebridge and Colindale depots.

Colindale, known as Hendon until the merger with Central Area in 1951, was a notable location in trolleybus history in Britain, as it was the place that witnessed one of the earliest experiments in trolleybus operation. In 1909, two years before trolleybuses made their public appearance in service in Leeds and Bradford, a single-deck trolleybus was operated in Hendon depot to demonstrate its potential to members of the Municipal Tramways Association, who were then meeting in London. In later years Colindale depot was to be famous for a much less positive development — behind the depot the scrapmen of George Cohen were to be employed dismantling the bulk of London's withdrawn trolleybus fleet.

Linking Canons Park and Barnet, via Cricklewood, Golders Green and Finchley, the 645 was converted to trolleybus operation on 2 August 1936. Part of its route — from Cricklewood to Edgware — represented the MET's first new electric tramway as opposed to converted horse tram routes. Inherited by the LPTB in 1933 the service was renumbered 45 before the conversion to trolleybus operation.

Whilst logic would indicate that service 660, from Hammersmith to North Finchley, largely replaced ex-MET tram route 60, this was not the case as the tram route linked North Finchley with Paddington via Cricklewood. The original route 6

Hammersmith to Acton on 5 April 1936. This shortlived service, operated from Acton depot, until 5 July 1936 when it was linked with (and renumbered) 666 to provide a Hammersmith-Edgware service. The 660 reappeared on 2 August 1936 for the Hammersmith-North Finchley service that was to last almost exactly 25 years.

The 662, from Sudbury to Paddington, was the only service that passed Stonebridge depot. It was another ex-MET tram route that was converted to trolleybus operation, this time on 23 August 1936. The withdrawal of services from the 662 in January 1962 removed the trolleybus from its final central terminus. Finally, in this stage, the 666, from Edgware to Hammersmith, was also converted. This largely replaced another ex-MET tram service. It was, however, not destined to have a long life as full service, being reduced to peak hours only shortly after its introduction. It was only the abandonment of the 664 during the service cuts of January 1959 that saw the 666 restored to all-day status.

Route Nos	Terminals	Replacement route	Type of Vehicle	Remarks
645	Canons Park-Barnet	245	RM	292, 292A, 293 introduced
660	Hammersmith-North Finchley	260	RM	
662	Paddington-Sudbury	18	RM, RT	
666	Hammersmith-Edgware	266	RM	
The following bus routes were amended: 2, 18B, 52A, 142				

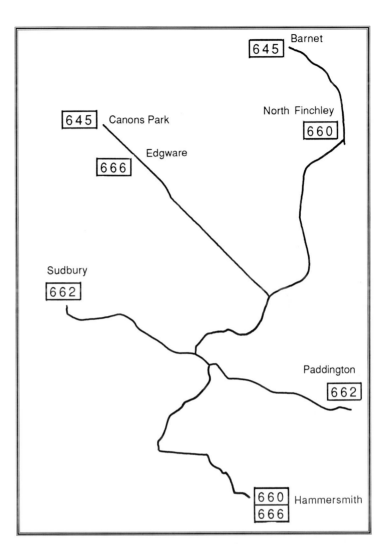

Left:
The handsome lines of the 'L3' class are evident in this view of No 1502 turning at the Barnet terminus of the 645 on 7 June 1960. The thicker window frames immediately behind the driver's cab and on the corresponding upper deck bay carry the cables from the trolley poles to the motors. The poster was rather appropriate at the time, as the author was about to hitch-hike to Scotland for his first visit north of the border.

Below left:
On the next day, during the trip north a visit to Leeds to see an ex-LT 'Feltham' tram proved fruitless as the last had been withdrawn in November the previous year, but Newcastle on the following afternoon was more successful as a BUT virtually identical to the postwar London 'Q1s' was encountered. Ledgard

Below:
RTL128, on the 28, and 'L3' No 1454, on the 660, are seen at Golders Green on 26 November 1960.

Left:
2 January 1962 saw London enveloped in some of the heaviest snow to fall on the suburbs for many years. The sun contrived to burst through for a few seconds in the afternoon, highlighting the evidence of the blizzard 'N1' No 1584 had battled through to reach Paddington Green. It is seen here turning to return to Stonebridge depot.

Below left:
In the forecourt of Stonebridge depot 'N1s and 'N2s', plus an RT, stand in the snow whilst ....

Above right:
... in the yard at the back of the depot more 'N1s' and 'N2s' wait to take up duty for the last time as the evening rush hour approaches.

Centre right:
Routemasters are seen arriving at Stonebridge on 2 January 1962 ready to take-over from the trolleybuses on the following morning. These buses were not new, being numbered in the 4xx series, and had been transferred from elsewhere after a spell in use as training vehicles.

Below right:
I can recall clearly riding along Burnt Oak Broadway in the autumn of 1961 in a Colindale 'N1' and wondering if it could really be true that this perfectly modern, smooth riding vehicle, and all its brothers, would shortly be consigned to the scrapheap. Unlike contemporary prewar diesel buses, which the trolleybuses had outlived by many years, the latter showed little sign of their age. There were few rattles or squeaks, there was no body sag, and the upholstery and interior fittings, if hardly pristine, were by no means shabby. They were certainly in vastly better shape than the last RTs operating in the late 1970s. But scrapped they were. Behind Colindale depot was a large expanse of waste ground and it was here that most London trolleybuses met their end.

Above:
On 22 April 1961 the yard at Colindale included these ex-Wood Green 'H1s', 'K1s' and 'K2s'. When the Bexleyheath trolleybuses were scrapped at Charlton a number of them still possessed their route and number blinds but, by this stage of the replacement scheme, the souvenir hunters had got themselves organised and there is not a blind to be seen.

Below:
In death as in life: ex-Edmonton 'K1s', 'K2s' and 'K3s' await their fate on 2 November 1961, still together as they had been for the previous 20 years in service.

It all came to an end on Wednesday 9 May 1962. Since then no trolleybus has run under the wires in the London area. But we have not quite reached journey's end yet and we have still to look at the particularly interesting last years of trolleybus operation in that part of southwest London where it had all begun three decades earlier.

It had originally been London Transport's intention to retain the 'Q1s' and the more or less self-contained group of routes they served until the end of the 1960s, but the complications of keeping a relatively small group of electrically-powered vehicles with their ancillary equipment marooned in a sea of diesel militated against this and when buyers for the 'Q1s' were found in Spain it was decided to make the withdrawal of the Isleworth and Fulwell routes the final and 14th stage of the trolleybus conversion programme. None of the 'Q1s' survived in London service to the bitter end, all 127 being withdrawn between November 1960 and April 1961. All but two had reached Spain by the end of the year. To replace them, and thus become the last operational trolleybuses in London, 'K1s' were sent to Isleworth and 'L3s' to Fulwell.

Farewell to London's Trolleybuses

The
Final Stronghold

Below:
The final nail in the London trolleybus coffin was the sale of the 'Q1s' to Spain. Here No 1830 is seen being loaded for its journey. In Spain, this was one of a number of 'Q1s' to operate in Pontevedra. Ian Allan Library

Left:
Earlier we touched on the arrival of the last new vehicles during the years 1948-52. There were 127 of these 'Q1' class trolleybuses and here we see No 1838, built in December 1948, pausing at Tolworth on 26 February 1961 to set down a very 1960s lady and a more or less timeless young fisherman (who was presumably back from trying his luck in the River Thames at Hampton Court where No 1838 had started its journey). Whilst the close family likeness with the later prewar classes, particularly the 'L3s' and 'P1s', is instantly obvious, there are differences. The 'Q1s' were six inches wider; the nearside windscreen was fixed; viewed side-on there was one window less (five instead of six); and, instead of the muscle-building snap window catches, the 'Q1s' had wind up windows like the contemporary RT-type. The bodies were built by Metro-Cammell. The chassis was the work of what at first sounded like a new manufacturer — British United Traction (or BUT as it was generally known). However, although BUT was emblazoned on the hubs, other parts were stamped or embossed AEC. BUT was merely the name of the selling organisation set up by Leyland and AEC and, although the 'Q1' chassis was designated 9641T, it was little different to the familiar AEC 664T. The 77 'Q1s' of the 1948 batch were all allocated to the original trolleybus depot, Fulwell, and took over routes 601-605. They stayed at Fulwell throughout their London careers.

Centre left:
The final 'Q1' of the 'HYM'-registered series was delivered in March 1949. Three years later delivery began of the very last batch of London trolleybuses. Identical in all respects to their predecessors, the 'LYH' batch was sent to Fulwell to work the 667, to Isleworth for the 657 and to Hanwell to work alongside the 'F1s' on the 607. No 1875 stands at the Shepherds Bush terminus of the 657 whilst Hammersmith and Hanwell 'F1s' ease past on 8 July 1960. Both the family likeness and the differences between these 1937 vintage and November 1952 vehicles are evident, although it is the former which are surely the most striking. When one thinks of the differences between contemporary diesel buses and coaches — the STL and the RT or the 10T10 and the RF — then the continuity in style throughout the entire production run of the London trolleybus from November 1935 to December 1952 is indeed remarkable.

Lower left:
The brief period when 'Q1s' and 'L3s' worked together is captured in this view at the Wimbledon terminus on 1 March 1961. 'Q1' No 1835, which would be withdrawn the following month, is working the 605 whilst 'L3' No 1443 sets off on the 604 to Hampton Court. Two months later No 1835 would be taking up duty in Zaragoza, whilst No 1443 would remain in operation from Fulwell until the last day of trolleybus operation in London.

Above:
'K1' No 1113 passes some typically-ornate late-Victorian London suburban architecture at Kew Bridge whilst on its way from Hounslow to Shepherds Bush on 26 October 1961.

Left:
The 657 was the only trolleybus route which passed Chiswick works. RT2998's learner driver turns carefully into the works for his lunch break whilst 'K1' No 1118, working back out of service from Shepherds Bush, slips past on the inside on 4 April 1961.

Above left:
Isleworth depot needed 25 vehicles to work the 657. A fair number of them are seen at rest inside the depot on 28 March 1962.

Left:
Four days before the end, on 5 May 1962, 'K1s' Nos 1113 (again) and 1061 gaze down on an ancient Austin passing their Hounslow terminus. Leslie Sandler

Above:
Spring breaks on 5 May 1962 outside St Mary's church, Ferry Road, Teddington as 'L3' No 1419 is chased by a Standard 8 convertible. For No 1419 summer will never come. Leslie Sandler

Right:
Two forms of electrically-powered street transport are seen in Hammersmith on 22 April 1962. 'L3' No 1386 may be the faster but the milk float had the last laugh for such vehicles are still a common sight in London more than three decades after the trolleybus has vanished. Leslie Sandler

Above left:
*Seen from the top deck of an Isleworth 'K1', Fulwell 'L3'
No 1441 approaches Kew Bridge and the ornate chimney of
the famous pumping station on 26 October 1961.*

Above:
*No 1426 turns at the Hampton Court terminus of the 657 on
26 February 1961. The entrance gates to Cardinal Wolsey's
palace are to the right of the trolleybus, above the Ford Anglia.*

Left:
*Several types, other than 'L3s', were sent to Fulwell in the
last few months of its career as a trolleybus depot, although if
any worked a scheduled service it was only in an emergency.
One which was certainly still operational on 26 October
1961 (even though it is officially recorded as having been
withdrawn in July that year) was the last 'L1' No 1369. It is
seen here under trade plates in the forecourt of Fulwell
depot, in front of the handsome depot buildings which dated
of course from the tramway days. There is no doubting that
trams once ran where No 1369 now stands.*

Below:
Four 'L3s' are pictured at Fulwell on 26 October 1961.

Above right:
*No 1524 passes under the distinctive support arms at
Tolworth on the service road alongside the remarkably empty
Kingston bypass on 5 May 1962. Leslie Sandler*

Right:
*Country Area RT1616, working on the 406a, passes 'L3'
No 1443 heading for Tolworth in Kingston town centre.
Ahead of the RT is the inevitable single-decker, a type which
has always been prolific in the Kingston area; in this case it
is an RF-type on the 216. The date is 26 October 1961.*

The final stage of the abandonment of London's trolleybus network occurred in early May 1962. Originally the £10 million conversion programme had been scheduled to take 13 stages with the remaining network of routes surviving until 1969/70. However, with the sale of the 'Q1s' the final withdrawal occurred within six months of Stage Thirteen.

This final stage was to affect seven routes in southwest London. Six of the routes were served from the original trolleybus depot at Fulwell, whilst the seventh, the 657 from Shepherds Bush to Hounslow was the preserve of Isleworth depot. It is interesting to note that, as the sections of the 657 and 667 from Young's Corner to Shepherds Bush and Hammersmith were also parts of London's first electric tram routes (opening in April 1901), these routes could claim the distinction of possessing electric street transport for the longest period in the Metropolis — a total of more than 61 years.

The 601, which ran from Twickenham to Tolworth via Kingston, originated with London United Tramways. Between 1902 and 1906 a series of tram routes in the Twickenham and Kingston area was opened and these formed the basis for the LUT's initial trolleybus conversions. Although powers were not formally obtained until 1930, the LUT had experimented with trolleybuses in Wimbledon eight years earlier. When inaugurated in May 1931 the original route, numbered appropriately service No 1, ran from Twickenham to Teddington — a distance of some 2.5 miles. The route was soon extended to Kingston during June 1931 and to Tolworth the next month. A final extension, to the Kingston bypass, opened in July 1933 under the aegis of the newly-created LPTB.

The 602 to The Dittons and the 603 to Tolworth were linked services in as much as the 602 operated around the Kingston Loop in an anticlockwise direction and the 603 in a clockwise direction. Again the origins of the routes lay in ex-LUT electric tram routes and both had been converted to trolleybus operation on 29 July 1931. The terminus at Tolworth was unusual in possessing reinforced concrete, rather than the more usual steel, traction columns.

The next place to receive trolleybuses was the location of the early LUT experimental operation — Wimbledon. Originally LUT tram route No 71 and initially trolleybus service No 4 when inaugurated on 2 September 1931, the 604

Farewell to London's Trolleybuses
Stage... 14
8/9 May 1962

Above left:
Bought in 1958 with the dismantling of the trolleybus overhead in mind but, at this date (6 May 1962), still helping maintain it is AEC Mercury tower-wagon No 1077Q. It was eventually sold in 1964. Leslie Sandler

Below left:
And so we come to the final day — 8 May 1962. Perhaps the nicest touch was the bringing out from retirement of the original 'Diddler' No 1. It is seen here, some days earlier, posed alongside 'L3' No 1419 at Fulwell. Leslie Sandler

linked Hampton Court with Wimbledon via Kingston. The construction of the tram route to Wimbledon (with its extension to Merton that later passed to the LCC) represented the final stage in the construction of the LUT tramway network. The second route to serve Wimbledon — the 605 to Twickenham — was a bit of a mystery. First operated some time in 1932 as LUT route No 5, it was originally a Saturdays Only service. A weekday service between Twickenham and Malden was established in early 1940 with peak hours extension to Wimbledon. The service became throughout on weekdays in December the same year. The ex-LUT routes Nos 1 to 5 were renumbered 601-5 in August 1935.

The final two routes to be converted at this time could lay claim to being operated over two stretches of road that had had electric street transport longer than any other thoroughfares in London — the links from Young's Corner to Shepherds Bush (on the 657) and that to

Hammersmith (on the 667). The 657 had its origins in a horse tram route opened in stages from Shepherds Bush to Kew Bridge in the 1880s. Electrification and the extension to Hounslow came in the early 1900s as part of the LUT network. The Hounslow tram service was numbered 57, thus becoming 657 on conversion to trolleybus operation on 27 October 1935. The same day saw the conversion of another ex-LUT tram route from Hammersmith to Fulwell. The new trolleybus service was extended beyond Fulwell to link up with the existing Hampton Court service — thus fulfilling a proposal dating from the early 1900s when the tramway was initially constructed. Prior to its closure to

trolleybus operation after Stage Eight, Hanwell depot provided a number of extras for use on Bank Holidays to supplement the vehicles drawn from Fulwell depot.

Although 'L3' No 1521 had the honour of operating the final public service — and was later presented by the scrap merchant George Cohen to the Historic Commercial Vehicle Club for preservation as a result — the vehicle that most people recall from the final day was the reappearance of 'Diddler' No 1, which had been in Fulwell depot since March 1962 to check that it was capable of carrying out a final run. No 1521 later passed to the London Trolleybus Preservation Society.

Route Nos	Terminals	Replacement route	Type of Vehicle	Remarks
601	Tolworth-Twickenham	281	RM	
602	The Dittons-Kingston Hill	282	RM	
603	Tolworth-Kingston Hill	283	RM	
604	Wimbledon-Hampton Court	131	RM, RT	
605	Wimbledon-Twickenham	285	RM	
657	Shepherds Bush-Hounslow	117	RM	
667	Hammersmith-Hampton Court	267	RM	

The following bus routes were amended: 90B, 116, 152

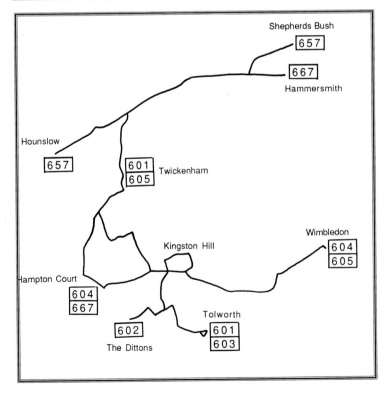

Above right:
No 1 made a ceremonial run on the last day, 8 May 1962, with invited guests from Fulwell over the 657 route to Twickenham, thence over the 601 — London's first trolleybus route — to Kingston, where it is seen here passing the bus garage watched by large crowds. In place of the 601 blinds it carried when first brought out of retirement, it bore the inscription 'London's Last Trolleybus 8 May 1962'.
Lens of Sutton

Right:
Its run complete, No 1 is seen here being towed back to Clapham Museum under the protection of a vigilant policeman.
Michael Dryhurst

Above:

Not surprisingly, the local press made much of the end of the London trolleybus system. Under the headline 'Sentimental Journey' the Wimbledon Borough News wrote 'London's last trolleybus was given a magnificent send off by hundreds of people outside Wimbledon Town Hall on Tuesday night... Dozens of people had waited for hours for the honour of a seat on the last bus and many were disappointed. Almost all the sightseers had cameras and flashguns.' Mike Beamish

Left:

The very last trolleybus was 'L3' No 1521. In the afternoon it had conveyed various dignitaries on the Richmond Park loop. One of these was Alan Townsin, Editor of Buses Illustrated, who wrote in the July 1962 edition 'There is little doubt that the changeover to motor buses is justified on economic grounds. The trolleybus itself does not, evidently, differ greatly from the bus in running costs but the maintenance of the overhead wiring adds considerably to them. It is, however, difficult to be dogmatic about costs and it is remarkable how different a picture sometimes appears to emerge when cost figures are being used to justify a particular line of action... it is useless to pretend that the diesel bus is as quiet, vibration-free or lacking in fumes as the trolleybus.' He goes on to comment 'despite the ageing fleet, the vehicles were generally kept in very smart condition,' something all of us who knew these often more than 20-year-old vehicles noted. It is remarkable how well they survived the rigours of war whilst the motor bus fleet was generally in a pretty sorry state, much of it having to be extensively refurbished to keep it operational even for only a couple or so more years' service.

Right:
Not the least remarkable aspect of the jollifications was that the driver of the last trolleybus was no less than 70 years old. 'Mr Albert West, the oldest driver on the staff at Fulwell, was besieged for ten minutes by photographers and autograph hunters. Mr West said he was sorry to see the trolleybus go, but he enjoyed the new Routemaster buses.' Albert West and conductor Ronald Gadsby. Another headline on an inside page had a very familiar ring about it: 'Curate of St Luke's, Wimbledon Park, complains of sex films and pornography'. Presumably he would not have approved of Jerry Lee Lewis who was appearing on stage that week at the Majestic, Mitcham Fair Green. I digress — but it is impossible not to do so when thumbing through old newspapers!
London Transport

Below:
Inside the last 657 from Isleworth depot. London Transport

Left:
The last service bus ran smoothly and when the bus reached Fulwell depot it was greeted by a huge crowd of bus drivers and conductors who escorted it into the depot. Here the souvenir hunters got to work and the vehicle lost quite a few of its accessories.

Above:
The handsome brick façade of Fulwell depot, or rather garage, is little changed from its tramway, let alone trolleybus, days. A Carlyle-bodied Dennis Dart is pictured working the R68, successor to a section of trolleybus replacement route 267, and two Metrobuses are on the 71 and 267, which replaced trolleybus route 667, at Fulwell on 13 December 1993.

Centre right
Sitting directly under the flight path for Heathrow it was perhaps appropriate that as London Transport gradually took over the former BEA (British Airways) front-entrance Routemasters, many of them were stored at Fulwell. M83 on the trolleybus-replacement route 267 stands beside a 1967-built British Airways RM at Fulwell in May 1979.

Right:
The existing route 131 from Walton to Kingston was extended to Wimbledon to cover trolleybus route 604. Although Titans had previously always been associated with East London, Westlink has recently brought a number into use for the heavily-trafficked 131. One of these, T912, is pictured at Wimbledon on 13 December 1993.

Above:

In Kingston, single-deckers are even more prolific today than they were 30-odd years ago. Where we saw 'Diddler' No 1 making its ceremonial last journey a London & Country National is caught approaching two Westlink Metroriders poking their noses out of the bus station into the rain.

Below:

A few pages earlier we saw an RT on the 406a passing an 'L3' trolleybus in Kingston. Routemasters took over both routes but these were themselves, in the fullness of time, replaced by one-man operated double and single-deckers. Great was the surprise in the winter of 1993 when London & Country's recently acquired (and only) Routemaster, RM1183, suddenly appeared on the 406. By a fascinating coincidence this was one of the batch delivered to Fulwell to replace the trolleybuses and is seen here passing the Railway Tavern, Surbiton, on a road where trolleybus routes 601/602/603 once ran. The date is 18 December 1993.

With the final demise of the trolleybus in London, work proceeded rapidly to remove the final vestiges of trolleybus operation. The overhead was gradually retrieved and 50 of the remaining 90-odd trolleybuses had passed to George Cohen for scrapping by the end of June. The last trolleybuses were transferred to the scrapyard during July 1962. These included eight 'N1s' and 'N2s' that had been retained temporarily by London Transport pending a possible sale to Spain. In the event the deal fell through and the eight — Nos 1637/41/53/55-59 — were to be the final trolleybuses to be scrapped at Colindale. In a gesture, George Cohen passed the last trolleybus in service, No 1521, over to the HCVC and later it was transferred to the London Trolleybus Preservation Society.

Although London may have bade farewell to the trolleybus, it was still possible to travel on a London trolleybus in Britain — No 260 was to appear on tour at a number of British systems (having also been rescued from the scrapman — and in Spain where a number of the ex-LT 'Q1s' continued to serve their new owners well into the 1970s. The survival of these vehicles was to lead to one of the more ambitious trolleybus preservation schemes when, in the mid-1970s, the British Trolleybus Society launched an appeal to repatriate one of those exported.

Farewell to London's Trolleybuses

Aftermath

The initial choice, No 1830 at Vigo, proved impossible due to vandalism, but the appeal was eventually to succeed with sister 'Q1' No 1812 in mid-1976. The return of No 1812 brought to nine the number of preserved London trolleybuses.

Below:
So what is left? The remaining trolleybuses — the 'L3s' from Fulwell and the 'K1s' from Isleworth — were soon broken up and burned.

Above:
However, this wasn't quite the end. From the earliest times, long before the preservation movement as we know it today got under way, London Transport had taken a responsible attitude to preservation. Consequently it set aside four examples which, small though this number was, did a pretty good job of representing the London trolleybus throughout its development. Representing the earlier standard vehicle is No 260, seen here at Brighton at the end of one of the early Historic Commercial Vehicle Club runs from London. Originally preserved by London Transport in 1959 (and displayed at Clapham), within two years it had passed into the hands of private preservationists (via the same George Cohen that had scrapped so many of its brothers). This picture demonstrates one of the problems of preservation for, when you have obtained your trolleybus, where on earth do you run it? No 260, a 'C2' class MCW-bodied AEC built in July 1936 and withdrawn in September 1959, had of course to be towed all the way to London and back on this occasion. During the 1960s No 260 was a familiar sight around the country as other towns and cities bade farewell to the trolleybus. V. C. Jones/IAL

Above right:
Most of the exported 'Q1s' were destined to have a further decade of service in Spain, but by the early 1970s withdrawals had started to take their toll. The British Trolleybus Society organised an appeal to repatriate one for display at the Sandtoft Transport Centre. No 1812 was ultimately the vehicle chosen and it is pictured here at the museum showing clearly many of the modifications undertaken for operation in Spain.

Centre right:
On the whole, the paths of London trolleybuses and donkeys did not cross all that often. However, in Ireland, it's a bit

different as 'K2' No 1348 has here found out. This all-Leyland, dating from June 1939, was withdrawn in July 1961 when most of the Wood Green and Walthamstow routes were converted to Routemaster operation and, in April 1962, it took the ferry to Dun Laoghaire. From there it was towed to Castleruddery, deep in rural County Wicklow, the home of the Transport Museum Society of Dublin. This organisation, with Michael Corcoran at its head, has, on a shoestring budget, managed to preserve a wonderful collection of vehicles from both sides of the Irish Sea. Shortage of covered space has meant that many of them have had to survive as best they may outside and, as it can be seen, No 1348 looks a bit the worse for wear. This photograph was taken in 1976, but the acquisition since then of a new covered museum at Howth, in the northern suburbs of Dublin, has been a great boon to the society.

Below right:
Another exile is 'H1' No 796. A Metro-Cammell-bodied Leyland, dating from February 1938 and withdrawn from Edmonton depot in November 1959, No 796 sailed away to France 11 months later and is pictured here in the transport museum in Paris. It stands beside one of the open-platform Renaults, of a slightly earlier vintage, which were such a feature of Paris streets for several decades, another London exile (a roof-box RT-type) and a Paris double-decker (an experiment which, for reasons best known to the Parisians themselves, the locals did not take to). No 796 has been kept under cover and is in precisely the condition in which it was withdrawn, perfectly serviceable and presentable but well-used. One has only to sit on its familiar upholstery to be instantly transported back to the Tottenham Court Road or Stamford Hill of the 1950s; it requires no great effort of the imagination to feel the characteristic slight jerk as it pulls away, the hum of the motors, the swish of the wheels and the drumming of the trolley poles on the roof as it picks up speed.

Left:

Nevertheless, all that is imagination. If you want to experience the real thing then you will have to journey to an even less likely setting than a former Paris bus garage, to the outskirts of the Suffolk seaside resort and port of Lowestoft. I'd been to the East Anglian Transport Museum several times but my latest visit came only after I had virtually finished the text and gathered together the illustrations for this book. I had got used to thinking that for all the vivid memories the photographs evoked and the nostalgia of the text, everything to do with the trolleybus belonged in the past, indeed more than 30 years into the past, hard as it may have been to believe that not since 1962 had I watched and travelled on the 'K1s' and 'L3s' going about their business in southwest London. Then one cold, cloudless Saturday afternoon in February 1994, Keith Farrow of the London Trolleybus Preservation Society, an author of several books on the complexities of overhead wiring, slid back the doors at Carlton (I've just corrected that from Charlton, a real Freudian slip — with lace trimmings!) Colville, and there stood 'Q1' No 1768, an extra bound for Isleworth depot, whilst alongside was 'L3' No 1521 scheduled, as it had been for so many years in the 1940s and 1950s, to work through the East End on the 567 from Aldgate to East Ham town hall. Behind them was 'C2' No 260 and a Newcastle representative of the northeast's version of the 'Q1'. And thus I was reminded through the efforts of the splendid band of volunteers at Carlton Colville, one of the friendliest bunch of enthusiasts it has been my pleasure to meet, that not only does

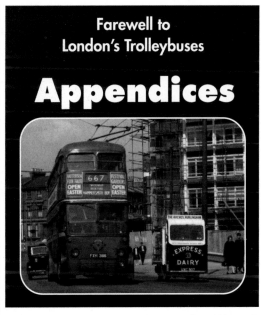

Farewell to London's Trolleybuses

Appendices

the London trolleybus survive but that it is still possible to ride on the big six-wheelers and experience again their unique ambience as they click and swish beneath the overhead.

Closure of Depots

Depot	Date	Code
Acton	26 May 1937	-
Wandsworth	30 September 1950	-
Bexleyheath	3 March 1959	BX
Carshalton	3 March 1959	CN
Leyton (Lea Bridge)	14 April 1959	LB
Hackney (Clapton)	14 April 1959	CT
Bow	18 August 1959	BW
Ilford	18 August 1959	ID
Poplar	10 November 1959	PR
Walthamstow	26 April 1960	WW
West Ham	26 April 1960	WH
Hammersmith	19 July 1960	HB
Holloway (Highgate)	25 April 1961	HT
Edmonton	18 July 1961	EM
Stamford Hill	18 July 1961	SF
Wood Green	7 November 1961	WN
Finchley	2 January 1962	FY
Hendon (Colindale)	2 January 1962	CE
Stonebridge	2 January 1962	SE
Fulwell	8 May 1962	FW
Hounslow (Isleworth)	8 May 1962	IH

Trolleybus Withdrawals

Before Stage One (118 vehicles)

B2	95,107
C2	184-94, 196, 198, 212, 215-20, 232, 237, 248, 275, 280
C3	284, 293, 304, 316, 324, 328, 330, 339, 348, 357, 359, 361, 362, 365, 367-69, 371, 372, 376, 377, 381-83
D2	389, 406, 426, 429, 454, 457, 469, 479, 481, 483, 489, 494, 495
D3	496, 519, 529, 535, 537-44, 552,
E1	556, 557, 559, 572
E2	604, 605, 609
H1	783, 817-20, 823-28, 861, 864, 888, 900, 904
J1	926, 944
J2	956, 984
K1	1128, 1247, 1257, 1285, 1292
N1	1565
K3	1690
SA1	1722-26, 1728, 1729

After Stage One (100 vehicles)

B1	65-70, 73-93
B2	97, 98
C3	335, 340, 344, 349, 352, 370, 375, 379
D2	388, 390-93, 395-97, 399, 401, 402, 404, 405, 407-17, 419, 423-25, 427, 430-32, 434, 439-42, 444, 451, 468, 470-76, 480
D2	491, 492
D3	553
F1	655, 711, 729
H1	766, 784, 786, 789, 790, 799, 804, 808, 809

Between Stages One and Two (two vehicles)

F1	711
H1	813

After Stage Two (84 vehicles)

D2	400, 420-22, 433, 436-38, 443, 445, 446, 449, 450, 452, 453, 455, 456, 458-67, 477, 478, 482
D3	499, 504, 507, 510, 511, 520, 521, 524, 536, 545, 547, 549, 551
H1	821, 822, 830-49, 851-60, 862, 863, 869, 871, 872, 877, 879, 882
K1	1123

Between Stages Two and Three (19 vehicles)

E3	663, 635, 641, 643
F1	675, 688, 735
H1	802, 894, 897, 901, 903
J2	1018
K1	1260
K2	1185, 1324, 1342
L3	1438
K3	1694

After Stage Three (108 vehicles)

C2	208, 231, 236, 241, 244, 245, 251, 252, 258, 260, 262, 271, 273, 276, 281
C3	285-92, 294-301, 303, 305-07, 309-11, 322, 325, 326, 329, 331, 334, 337, 338, 347, 373
E1	554, 555, 558, 560, 562, 566, 567, 571, 573-75, 578, 602
E2	619, 621, 626
E3	629
F1	701
H1	866, 873, 895
J1	917, 941
J2	1010
K1	1088
L3	1423
K3	1685
SA1	1727, 1731
SA2	1734-46
SA3	1747-64

Between Stages Three and Four (eight vehicles)

C3	318
H1	885, 899
J2	985, 1021
K1	1056
K2	1319
N2	1650

After Stage Four (62 vehicles)

C2	272, 277, 279
C3	302, 308, 312-17, 319-21, 323, 327, 332, 336, 345, 346, 354, 356, 363
E1	561, 563-65, 576, 579-86
E2	611
H1	796
J1	905-08, 910, 912, 913, 918, 919, 921, 923, 924, 927-32, 934
N1	1555, 1587

Between Stages Four and Five (12 vehicles)

E1	577
E2	614, 624
F1	672, 750
H1	801
J2	958, 987
K1	1064
L1	1368
L3	1416, 1459

After Stage Five (80 vehicles)

E1	587-94, 596, 597, 599, 603
E2	606-08, 610, 612, 613, 615-18, 620, 625, 627, 628
F1	722, 734, 741, 745

H1	765, 785, 788, 793, 794, 797, 798, 800, 805-07, 811, 850, 874, 883, 884, 886, 887, 889, 890, 893
J1	936-40, 942, 943, 945-51
J2	955, 957, 959, 961, 963, 967, 986, 988, 989, 991-4, 997, 1001

Between Stages Five and Six (25 vehicles)

H1	898, 902
J1	952
J2	960, 962, 966, 968, 969, 973, 974, 976, 977, 979, 983, 990, 995, 999, 1013, 1015
K1	1086, 1102, 1113, 1329
K2	1249
P1	1699

After Stage Six (111 vehicles)

E2	622
H1	755-64, 767-82, 814, 815, 865, 867, 868, 870, 875, 876, 878, 880, 881, 891, 892, 896
J1	911, 933, 935
J2	964, 965, 970-72, 975, 978, 980-82, 996, 998, 1000, 1002-09, 1011, 1012, 1014, 1016, 1017, 1019, 1020, 1022-29
J3	1030, 1031, 1033-39, 1041, 1043, 1046
K2	1171, 1203, 1217, 1220, 1318
L3	1385, 1529
M1	1530-36, 1542, 1543, 1545, 1549, 1550

Between Stages Six and Seven (four vehicles)

K1	1106, 1265
L2	1376
L3	1418

After Stage Seven (71 vehicles)

F1	656-62, 670, 673, 674, 730, 746, 752
J3	1040, 1042, 1044, 1045, 1047-53
K1	1071, 1073, 1075, 1076, 1078, 1080, 1081, 1083, 1085, 1119-22, 1124, 1125, 1129, 1273, 1275, 1279
K2	1158-64, 1176, 1178, 1201, 1202, 1204, 1240, 1241, 1325, 1327, 1331, 1332
P1	1698, 1700, 1703, 1709, 1713, 1714, 1716, 1718, 1719, 1721

Between Stages Seven and Eight (20 vehicles)

F1	666, 667, 671, 678, 696, 702, 721, 731, 737, 743, 753
H1	816
K1	1069, 1070, 1100
K2	1157, 1212
M1	1537
N1	1562
P1	1717

After Stage Eight (70 vehicles)

F1	654, 663-65, 668, 669, 671, 676, 677, 679-86,

	689-95, 697, 699, 700, 702-10, 712-20, 723-28, 731-33, 736, 738-40, 742, 743, 747-49, 751, 753
K2	1157, 1162, 1164, 1204
Q1	1766

Between Stages Eight and Nine (six vehicles)

J3	1032, 1054
L1	1359
L3	1406, 1471
N1	1606

After Stage Nine (106 vehicles)

H1	829
K1	1153
K2	1317, 1320, 1328, 1330
L1	1355-58, 1360-64
L3	1410, 1454
M1	1538
Q1	1766, 1767, 1769-77, 1781-83, 1785, 1788, 1791, 1794, 1795, 1799, 1801-05, 1808-12, 1816, 1817, 1819, 1821-24, 1829, 1842-91

Between Stages Nine and Ten (21 vehicles)

K1	1065, 1066, 1068, 1138, 1266-68
K2	1173, 1190, 1354
L1	1366, 1367
L2	1371, 1372, 1374, 1375
L3	1382, 1388
M1	1538
N1	1599
N2	1645

After Stage Ten (144 Vehicles)

K1	1059, 1063, 1079, 1082, 1084, 1087, 1089-96, 1099, 1105, 1110, 1115, 1132, 1140-42, 1150, 1261, 1272, 1278, 1293, 1295, 1296, 1298, 1303
K2	1155, 1156, 1165-70, 1172, 1174, 1175, 1177, 1179-84, 1186-89, 1191-97, 1209, 1215, 1223, 1230, 1248, 1250, 1253, 1254, 1306, 1321, 1333
K3	1676, 1686, 1693
L1	1369
L2	954, 1370, 1373, 1377, 1378
L3	1440
M1	1541, 1542, 1551, 1552
N1	1560, 1566, 1574, 1577, 1581, 1589, 1595, 1601
P1	1697, 1701, 1702, 1704-08, 1710-12, 1715, 1720
Q1	1765, 1768, 1778-80, 1784, 1786, 1787, 1789, 1790, 1792, 1793, 1796-98, 1800, 1806, 1807, 1813-15, 1818, 1820, 1825-28, 1830-40

After Stage Eleven (82 vehicles)

K1	1055, 1097, 1105, 1108, 1109, 1111, 1112, 1127, 1130, 1131, 1133-37, 1145, 1148, 1151, 1152, 1255, 1256, 1264

K2	1198, 1205-08, 1211-14, 1216, 1218, 1219, 1221, 1224-29, 1231-38, 1242, 1243, 1245, 1305, 1307, 1310, 1314, 1315, 1335, 1336, 1338-41, 1343, 1346-50		1424, 1428, 1435, 1439, 1442, 1447, 1448, 1453, 1463, 1467, 1470, 1476, 1478, 1485, 1486-88, 1498, 1501, 1503, 1505, 1507-09, 1513, 1520, 1527
K3	1672, 1673, 1678, 1681, 1683, 1684, 1687-89, 1692, 1695	N1	1557, 1575, 1634
L3	1429	N2	1669
N2	1663		

After Stage Thirteen (105 vehicles)

Between Stages Eleven and Twelve (21 vehicles)

K1	1149, 1291, 1300
K2	1199, 1309, 1337, 1344, 1345
L3	1383, 1404, 1505
N1	1571, 1596
K3	1674, 1675, 1677, 1679, 1680, 1682, 1691, 1696

L3	1402, 1449-52, 1457, 1458, 1461, 1464-66, 1468, 1469, 1484, 1529
N1	1556, 1558, 1559, 1561, 1563, 1564, 1567-70, 1572, 1573, 1577-86, 1588, 1590, 1591, 1593-95, 1597, 1598, 1600, 1602-05, 1607-33, 1635-44
N2	1646-49, 1651, 1653-61, 1664-68

After Stage Twelve (95 vehicles)

K1	1062, 1072, 1098, 1116, 1147, 1154, 1258, 1259, 1262, 1263, 1269, 1277, 1280-82, 1284, 1286, 1287, 1289, 1291, 1294, 1297, 1299, 1301, 1302, 1304
K2	1199, 1200, 1210, 1239, 1246, 1251, 1252, 1308, 1311, 1312, 1313, 1316, 1322, 1323, 1334, 1351-54
L2	1373, 1377
L3	1384, 1389, 1391, 1392, 1398, 1400, 1403, 1408, 1409, 1412, 1414, 1415, 1417, 1420-22,

After Stage Fourteen (90 vehicles)

| K1 | 1057, 1058, 1060, 1061, 1074, 1077, 1101, 1103, 1104, 1107, 1113, 1114, 1117, 1118, 1126, 1143, 1144, 1146, 1270, 1274, 1276, 1283 |
| L3 | 1380, 1381, 1386, 1390, 1393-96, 1399, 1401, 1405, 1407, 1411, 1413, 1419, 1425, 1426, 1430-33, 1436, 1437, 1441, 1443-46, 1456, 1462, 1472-75, 1477, 1479, 1480, 1482, 1483, 1489-91, 1493-97, 1499, 1500, 1502, 1504, 1506, 1510-12, 1514-19, 1521-26, 1528 |

Preserved vehicles:

1, 260, 796, 1201, 1253, 1348, 1521, 1768, 1812

Transfers to Spain*:

Bilbao
1843/45/47/49/51/53/55/57/59/61/63/65/67/69/71/73/75/77/79/81/83/85/87/89/91
San Sebastian
1842/44/46/48/50/52/54/56/58/60/62/64/66/68/70/72/74/76/78/80/82/84/86/88/90
Pontevedra
1776/77/88-91/95/97-99/801/03/04/06/11/13/14/16/20/24/26/27/30/31
Corunna
1782/83/85/94/802/05/08/09/17/19/22/23
Corunna-Carballo
1766/67/69-74
Santander
1775/81/810/12/21/29
Tarragona
1792/93
Vigo
1765/78/80/84/87/96/800/07/15/25/28
Zaragoza
1779/86/818/32-40
Official locations; actual owners varied.